Discovering
SAINTS IN BRITAIN

John Vince

Shire Publications Ltd

CONTENTS

"For all the Saints
Who from their labours rest
Who Thee by Faith
Before the world confessed . . ."

Cover illustration by Rachel Lewis.

Printed in Great Britain by C. I. Thomas & Sons (Haverfordwest) Ltd,
Press Buildings, Merlins Bridge, Haverfordwest, Dyfed SA61 1XF.

INTRODUCTION

The story of saints in Britain stretches back to the earliest years of Christianity. An acquisitive age does not seem to have much regard for those who laboured for the Lord so many centuries ago, but their names remain and many are used in our day to day world. Some are so familiar that they pass unheeded from the lips—Bart's (St. Bartholomew's) and St. Thomas's have no need to be called hospitals; St. Leger has given his name to a horse race; and St. Pancras is a railway station.

In earlier ages when most people were illiterate, churches were then decorated with murals and statues to remind worshippers of the principal events of the New Testament and the lives of the saints who followed its teaching.

Over three hundred different saints are commemorated in our six thousand or so parish churches. The name of the Blessed Virgin Mary can be found over two thousand times but the names of nearly a hundred and fifty saints occur only once. There are four main sources of the saints' names appearing in this book: The New Testament; Continental Europe; Celtic Britain; and Anglo-Saxon Britain. About twenty five Biblical saints' names can be found but names from Celtic and Saxon sources seem to predominate among the remainder.

Representations of saints in glass, painting or sculpture have been listed below, but the brief notes merely indicate specimens that have come to my notice. Each short list is no more than a starting point for the enthusiastic hagiologist. References to the number of dedications concern English churches only.

Britons may have forgotten their saints, but the country abounds with reminders of their Christian witness.

ABBREVIATIONS

A. or Ab.	Abbot. Abbess.	Ev.	Evangelist.
Abp.	Archbishop.	H.	Hermit.
Arch.	Archangel.	K.	King.
.Ap.	Apostle.	M.	Martyr.
App.	Apostles.	MM.	Martyrs.
B.	Bishop.	P.	Pope.
b.	born.	Qu.	Queen.
C.	Confessor.	V.	Virgin.
D.	Doctor of the Church.	VV.	Virgins.
d.	died.	V.M.	Virgin and Martyr.
Emp.	Emperor.	W. or Wid.	Widow.

3

ST. ADRIAN (d. 710)   9th January

St. Adrian was an abbot and a companion of St. Augustine. He has no English dedications. He should not be confused with the martyr of the same name.

ST. AIDAN OF LINDISFARNE (d. 651)   31st August

Aidan was an Irish monk sent from the community of Iona to rescue the people of Northumbria from paganism. He established his church on the island of Lindisfarne (Holy Island) where he ruled as bishop for sixteen years. In Aidan's early years as bishop the King, Ostwald, often acted as his interpreter. Many legends were attached to Aidan. One records the attack launched by Penda upon Ostwald's stronghold at Bamburgh. Brushwood was piled around its—presumably wooden—walls. Aidan saw the smoke and his prayers effected a change in the wind so that the flames turned upon the attackers and the castle survived.

On the night Aidan died a humble shepherd boy (who later became St. Cuthbert) saw on the nearby hills a brilliant shaft of light shining from above, and Aidan's soul being transported heavenwards.

In Christian art Aidan is shown with a stag at his feet; calming a storm; extinguishing fire; and holding a lighted torch.

ST. ALBAN (b. 305)   17th June

St. Alban was the first English martyr. He was born in 305 at Verulam and his education was based on pagan teachings. An old priest sought shelter in Alban's home during the vigorous persecutions under Diocletian's rule and he. was responsible for converting Alban to the faith. To assist the priest's escape Alban exchanged clothes with the old man. For the part he played in helping the priest to escape Alban was sentenced to death.

The place of execution lay on the other side of the river Colne and the crowd proved to be too great for the narrow bridge over its waters. At the saint's command, so the legend says, the waters parted and the crowd crossed the river bed without getting wet. Alban was executed in the Roman manner with a sword, and the arms used by the bishop of St. Albans remind us of this circumstance.

The episcopal shield is described in heraldic language as follows: azure, a saltire, or, over all a sword erect in pale proper, pommelled and hilted of the second. In chief a celestial crown or. In layman's terms this means that the blue shield is charged with a golden diagonal cross. Over the cross is a vertical sword surmounted by a crown.

After Alban's death his place of burial was for a time forgotten, but it was rediscovered, in a vision, by the Mercian King Offa who was the founder of the present Abbey. During the middle ages Alban's shrine attracted many pilgrims, but after the dissolution of the monasteries its fabric was destroyed. The carefully restored shrine which visitors to the Abbey may now see was reconstructed from over two thousand fragments in 1872. Alban is engraved on the Delamere brass at St. Albans. He is also shown in a window at St. Mary's, Warwick. Eleven English churches are dedicated to him.

See also—Amphibalus.

ST. ALDHELM (640-709)   25th May
St. Aldhelm became Abbot of Malmesbury, Wilts, in about 675. There he pioneered monastic revival based on the Rule of St. Benedict and the abbey became a model for monasteries Aldhelm founded at Frome and Bradford-on-Avon. He built three churches in Malmesbury. In one of these a prayer by Aldhelm miraculously lengthened a rafter cut too short; elsewhere his staff is said to have taken root during a long sermon he preached! His literary style, though equally wordy, gained him an international reputation as a scholar. He wrote Christian songs in the language of the people. He became first bishop of Sherborne in 705. When he died in 709 he was buried at St. Michael the Archangel, Malmesbury. Four English churches are dedicated to him.

ALFRED (849-899)   26th October
Alfred the Great was the son of Ethelwulf, King of the West Saxons. He fought many fierce battles against the heathen Danish invaders.

As a young man Alfred was taken to Rome. He loved books and translated many Latin texts into English. Alfred's laws made it possible for his subjects to live peacefully together.

There are statues of Alfred at Winchester, Hants., and at his birthplace at Wantage, Oxon.

Although he was never canonized, the English Church celebrates his feast day.

ST. ALKMUND (774-819)   19th March
Alkmund was the son of the Northumbrian King Alcred.
He met his death at the hands of the Danes, but no details of
his martyrdom have survived. He was first buried at Lilleshall,
Salop, and soon afterwards transferred to Derby to become its
patron saint.

The church at Duffield (Derbys)—where the body was rested
on its journey—is understandably dedicated to him.

Eight old churches are dedicated to him—Atcham (Salop);
Aymestrey (Hereford); Bliburgh (Lincs.); Derby; Duffield
(Derbys.); Shrewsbury; Whitchurch and Wormbridge (Salop).

ST. ALPHAGE (952-1012)   19th April
Alphage was Bishop of Winchester and later Archbishop of
Canterbury. He was held for ransom and later murdered by the
Danes at Greenwich, where his church still stands. Four other
churches are also dedicated to him. He appears in a four-
teenth century window at Deerhurst, Glos.

ST. ALRED, AELRED, AILRED (1109-1167)   12th January
Alred was the son of a Saxon priest of Hexham. He became
Abbot at Revesby and later at Rievaulx. In 1163 he witnessed
the translation of Edward the Confessor to Westminster.

ST. AMPHIBALUS (4th Cent.)   22nd June
Amphibalus was the priest who was responsible for the
conversion of St. Alban. Soon after the protomartyr was
executed Amphibalus and his followers were captured—at
Redbourn (Herts.). There they were stoned and their bodies
buried in a field. About eight hundred years later the remains
of the saint were transferred to St. Albans where they received
a place of honour.

In St. Albans Abbey Amphibalus is represented bound to
a tree by his bowels while being scourged. During the fifteenth
century heraldic arms were often attributed to various saints.
The details of his "arms" are as follows: — a shield divided
into quarters each bearing a lion rampant. In the first and
fourth quarter the background is red and the lion gold. The
other two divisions have these colours reversed—or, in heraldic
terms, counterchanged.

ST. ANDREW (1st Cent.)   30th November
Andrew was an apostle. The tradition that he suffered on
a diagonal, or X-shaped, cross seems to have originated in the
middle ages. He is the patron saint of Scotland. About six

hundred churches are dedicated to him. The saltire cross is his usual emblem.

ST. ANSELM (c. 1033-1109) 21st April
He was Archbishop of Canterbury during the reign of Rufus and Henry I. In 1094 he consecrated Battle Abbey which William I, on the eve of Hastings (1066), had vowed to build.

ST. ANTONY OF EGYPT (d. 356) 17th January
St. Antony of Egypt is remembered for his long and austere life. Tradition credits him with an age of one hundred and five years.

The Cross of St. Antony is of ancient origin. It is sometimes known as an Egyptian cross owing to its use, as a symbol of life, by the ancient Egyptians. The Greeks called it a tau cross—after the Greek letter of that name. In early Christian art the cross of Calvary is also represented in this way.

Other emblems associated with St. Antony are a bell and a pig. The pig is supposed to have been his sole companion during his solitary meditations in the desert.

Only nine English churches are dedicated to St. Antony. He has also given his name to the two Cornish villages of— St. Antony-in-Roseland, and St. Antony-in-Meneage.

The Arms of the Friars of St. Antony (London) show a blue tau cross on a gold shield.

ST. AUDREY—see ETHELDREDA

ST. AUGUSTINE (d. 604) 26th May
Augustine was sent to England in 597 by Pope Gregory. His first meeting with the Saxon King Ethelbert of Kent took place in the open as the King wished to avoid being bewitched. Augustine converted Ethelbert and was later made, by the Pope, Primate of all England. During the rest of Augustine's life he tried to persuade the bishops of the Celtic Church to accept the Roman usage. He was responsible for introducing the Benedictine Order to England.

The symbol of his papal authority—the pallium—can still be seen on the arms of the See of Canterbury. This shows, on a blue shield, the Y-shaped cross pall over an archbishop's crozier.

ST. BARTHOLOMEW (1st Cent.) 24th August
St. Bartholomew was one of our Lord's apostles. He is mentioned in three of the Gospels, and in the Acts of the Apostles. Bartholomew is said to have carried the gospel into India.

7

The people of India in those days worshipped idols. Among his works Bartholomew healed the lunatic daughter of Polemius, a king, who became converted to the Christian faith. The priests who served the idols did not like Bartholomew's teaching. Fearing that their practices would be banned they went to Astrages, brother of King Polemius, to ask for his support. Astrages sent a thousand soldiers to capture Bartholomew and he suffered martyrdom by being flayed alive; his special emblem is a flaying knife.

Up to the fifteenth century each visitor to Crowland Abbey, Lincolnshire was presented with a silver knife on the saint's feast day. The abbots found that it was an expensive custom, and so it gradually fell into disuse.

St. Bartholomew's Hospital in London is named after him. More than one hundred and sixty churches are dedicated to him. At Fingest, Bucks. the churchwardens' wands are surmounted by flaying knives.

BEDE, THE VENERABLE (673-735)　　　　27th May
Bede is best remembered for his *History of the English Church and People* which is still in print! Most of his life was spent in Northumbria—at Jarrow or Monkwearmouth. He is the first known prose writer in the vernacular tongue.

ST. BEE (7th Cent.)　　　　31st October
The small Cumbrian village (St. Bees) preserves the name of a nun, St. Bega, who was probably Irish. Her name has been confused with another nun—Begu—who was mentioned by Bede and authorities frequently differ on the subject. Three churches are dedicated to her.

ST. BENEDICT BISCOP (628-690)　　　　12th January
At the age of twenty five he left the service of the Northumbrian King Oswy to enter the Church. He travelled six times to Rome and amassed the important libraries at Monkwearmouth and Jarrow upon which Bede's scholarship was founded.

ST. BIRINUS (BERIN) (7th Cent.)　　　　5th December
Birinus came to England in 633 A.D. and he is best remembered for his work in converting the people of Wessex to Christianity. After landing in Hampshire he eventually established his church in the Thames Valley—at Dorchester (Oxon.). This became his cathedral. In the Thames near the site of the present church Birinus baptised Cynegils, King of Wessex, in

the presence of St. Oswald.

Birinus was buried at Dorchester. Later the See was transferred to Winchester, and in 676 Bishop Heddi established his shrine there. In the thirteenth century the saint's body was found still at Dorchester and a shrine was built. This was destroyed at the Dissolution, but in 1964 the pieces were reassembled.

St. Birinus is sometimes shown walking across the sea carrying the Sacrament.

ST. BLAISE (4th Cent.)   3rd February

St. Blaise was a physician before he became Bishop of Sebaste in Asia Minor during the fourth century. He lived a simple and humble life. People would often seek his aid in time of need. One legend tells how, with a touch of his hand, he cured a child who had a fishbone lodged in his throat and was near to death. Another story records how his prayers restored a poor woman's pig which had been carried off by a wolf.

When Diocletian ordered the seizure of all Christians in 303, Blaise was arrested and brought before the governor of the province. He refused to sacrifice to idols and was hung on a gibbet while his body was torn with iron combs. When he was thrown into the river to drown Blaise is said to have walked upon the water until he reached the bank. His tormentors finally beheaded him. The iron comb became his symbol, and in mediaeval times the wool combers adopted Blaise as their patron saint.

Until the nineteenth century St. Blaise's feast day was celebrated in Bradford, Yorks., at seven yearly intervals. The wool workers would parade round the streets singing and dancing.

He is also patron saint of physicians and wax chandlers, and is sometimes confused with the other five saints who bear the same name.

During the middle ages the stumps of candles offered to him on his feast day were believed to be excellent cures for tooth ache.

Three English churches commemorate his name: St. Blazey, Cornwall; Haccombe, Devon; and Milton, Oxon. St. Blaise is also shown in Christchurch Cathedral, Oxford; at Ashton, Devon carrying his iron comb; and on the rood at St. Mary Steps, Exeter.

ST. BONIFACE (d. 754)   5th June

Boniface was born at Crediton, Devon in the late seventh

century. He received his early education at 'Nursling, Hants. When he was still a young man, he was summoned to Rome and was there created a bishop. Boniface laboured to convert the pagan hordes in Hesse and Thuringia. On the 5th June 754 he was slain by a group of heathens, and his followers buried him in the old cathedral at Fulda, Germany.

Several emblems are associated with him. One of the most common shows him with an axe felling Thor's oak (a symbol of paganism). Others include: a book pierced with a sword; a scourge (whip); a hand presenting him with a cross; and an axe with an oak tree.

A minor shrine containing one of the saint's bones was discovered late in the last century in a wall at Brixworth church, Northants.

ST. BOTOLPH (d. 655)   17th June

Botolph was a Saxon abbot and very little information concerning his life has survived. His principal memorial is to be found in the names of Boston, Lincs., where he is said to have founded his abbey, and of Botolph Claydon, Bucks. which was once in the diocese of Lincoln.

He appears in Christian art holding a church or monastery in his hand. Many saints are shown in this way and it is easy to confuse them with one another. If a name or other symbol is included this can often supply the vital clue to the figure's exact identity. A modern sculpture of this saint can be seen at St. Botolph, Bradenham, Bucks.

ST. BRICE (4th Cent.)   13th November

St. Brice was Bishop of Tours, in France, in the fourth century. He was a proud ambitious man and people began to dislike him. Eventually, false accusations were made against him. Caxton's *Golden Legend* records that to prove his innocence Brice carried burning coals in his vestment to the tomb of his predecessor St. Martin. This feat was accomplished without damage to his clothing.

St. Brice is represented carrying the burning coals either in his hand or vestments.

The only English church dedicated to this saint is at Brize Norton, Oxfordshire.

ST. BRITWALD (d. 731)   9th January

Britwald was a Benedictine monk who was abbot of Glastonbury and then of Reculver. He was buried at Canterbury.

ST. BRYNACH (7th Cent.)

One tradition of this remarkable saint records that he

sailed from Rome to Milford Haven on a rock. He released Fishguard from unclean, howling spirits which had made the place difficult to live in.

ST. CATHERINE (4th Cent.) 25th November

St. Catherine lived in the fourth century. She was the daughter of the King of Cyprus. Legend records that she met her death at the hands of Emperor Maxentius in Alexandria.

As Catherine constantly refused to sacrifice to his gods, Maxentius commanded that four spiked wheels should be set up and that her body should be crushed between them.

St. Catherine was one of the most popular saints of the middle ages. There are eighty churches dedicated to her in England. They are situated as far apart as Crook, Cumbria, and Ventnor, Isle of Wight.

She is patroness of jurists, students, philosophers, millers, wagon makers, young women and teachers. Her usual symbol is a spiked wheel, but she may be shown holding a sword.

The College of St. Catherine, Oxford includes a spiked wheel in its arms. Other examples of her emblem may be found at Westhall, Suffolk; Lessingham, Norfolk, Combe-In-Teignhead, Devon; St. Osyth, Essex; Ludlow, Salop; and All Souls College, Oxford.

Catherine has also given her name to the villages of Catherington, Hants., and St. Catherine, Avon.

In the Church's calendar 25th November is set aside as her feast day. Children may more easily remember her as they light their catherine wheels on 5th November.

ST. CEDD (7th Cent.) 7th January

Cedd was St. Chad's brother. He became a bishop and founded the abbey at Lastingham, Yorks.

ST. CHAD (d. 672) 2nd March

St. Chad lived in England during the seventh century. He was probably the youngest of four brothers who all became eminent priests—viz. Cedd, Cynebil and Celin. Chad is often confused with his brother Cedd, Bishop of the East Saxons. We know, from Bede, that Chad was a pupil of Aidan. He became Bishop of Northumbria and later of Mercia. The Mercian bishopric had been established at Repton, Derbyshire, and Chad was responsible for its removal to Lichfield—the "Field of the Dead" where a thousand Christians are said to have been put to death. It was Chad's custom to go about on foot rather than on horseback and he acquired a reputation for humility. There are thirty-one churches dedicated to him in the midlands. The first church ever built in Shrewsbury was

11

named after him and it still contains an ancient effigy showing Chad in his robes.

There was a well of St. Chad at Lichfield and another in London. At one time the water was sold for 6d. a glass! The miracles which were said to derive from mixing dust from his shrine at Lichfield with water helped to make him the patron of medicinal springs. The name Chadwell, Essex, is derived from Chad's name.

KING CHARLES THE MARTYR (1600-1649)   30th January

After the Civil War Charles was subsequently imprisoned and then brought to trial by the Puritans. He was executed on 30th January 1649 in Whitehall. At the Restoration this day was kept as a public fast and special prayers were recited. Each year a wreath is laid at his statue at the end of Whitehall. Five English churches are dedicated to him.

ST. CHRISTOPHER (date uncertain)   25th July

The name Christopher comes from the Greek and means Christ bearer. The legend of the giant who, unknowingly, carried the Christ Child across the river is well known. Christopher can be found on memorial brasses—as at Weeke, Winchester, Hants. He also appears on a fresco at Cirencester, Glos. and there are many examples of his figure painted on the walls of churches, usually facing the south doorway, as at Little Missenden, Bucks. He is still a popular saint with motorists and other travellers to judge by the number of Christopher medallions that adorn motor vehicles. The spacemen who circled the moon in Apollo 8 carried St. Christopher emblems with them. Nine English churches are dedicated to him. See page 30.

ST. COLUMBA (520-697)   9th June

Columba was an Irish abbot and missionary. He founded the monastery on the lonely island of Iona.

ST. CUTHBERT (d. 687)   20th March

Cuthbert was a shepherd boy who, while tending his sheep on the hills above Melrose, saw in the night sky a vision of St. Aidan's soul being carried up to heaven. Nothing is known about Cuthbert's origins but following his vision he entered the monastery at Melrose. His austere way of life is remembered in the story of the otters. After a night long vigil of prayer standing up to his chin in the cold waters of the sea he returned to the shore to continue his devotions. Two otters then came out of the sea and licked his feet to restore warmth to his body.

Cuthbert's name is usually associated with the lonely island of Lindisfarne (Holy Island) where he lived in retreat following his retirement from Melrose. Shortly before his death he was created bishop, but he returned to his beloved island to die in 687. During the Danish invasion his body was removed to Durham where it remains. An old legend concerns the first church built there in the tenth century. The bearers of Cuthbert's body were guided to the place where the saint was interred by a maiden, looking for a lost cow.

ST. CUTHMAN (9th Cent.)   8th February
Cuthman was a shepherd boy who migrated from the West Country pulling his mother in a hand cart. When he reached Steyning, Sussex, the handles broke. He then built a church there as an act of thanksgiving. The story is told by Christopher Fry in his play *The Boy with the Cart* (1939).

ST. DAVID—DEWI SANT (6th Cent.)   1st March
St. David is the patron saint of Wales. He was an abbot and a bishop. His monastery stood at the place now called St. Davids, Pembs. Shakespeare made his emblem the leek (*Henry V*) instead of the usual dove. Twenty three churches are dedicated to him including Little and Much Dewchurch, Herefs.

ST. DEINIOL (7th Cent.)   10th December
Deiniol was Bishop of Bangor. His father, called Denooth by Bede, was abbot of Bangor Iscoed at the time of the Council of the Oak with Augustine (600—603).

ST. DUNSTAN (d. 988)   19th May
St. Dunstan was born of noble parents near the great monastery at Glastonbury, Somerset, in the tenth century. He entered the monastery as a young man and became a member of the religious order founded by St. Benedict. He was eventually elected abbot, and later became Archbishop of Canterbury.

He had many artistic abilities and spent much of his spare time working with his hands. He was an accomplished scribe, metal worker and musician.

The most popular legend concerning him tells how he vanquished the devil who came to tempt him. Dunstan was making a golden chalice for his church when the devil appeared. Dunstan instantly seized the fiend by the nose with his hot tongs, and held him fast. An old rhyme records the encounter:

Saint Dunstan so the story goes
once pulled the devil by the nose.

With red-hot tongs, which made him roar,
that he was heard three miles or more.

Dunstan became the patron saint of goldsmiths. His emblem is a pair of pincers.

Nineteen English churches are dedicated to him and a window at the Bodleian Library, Oxford shows Dunstan holding the devil with his pincers. At Ludlow, Salop, he is shown with his pincers and in Exeter Cathedral a roof boss portrays him as a harpist.

ST. EDMUND (d. 870)   20th November

Edmund was king in East Anglia during the Danish invasion which began in 866, and perished at the hands of Hingrar and Hubba, near Thetford. Edmund was tied to a tree and the Danes shot him with their arrows. The body was then decapitated. The saint's body and head were eventually recovered and interred at Bury St. Edmunds (a wolf is supposed to have carried the head to the searchers.)

The saint is often shown with arrows in his hand—at Ludham and Stalham in Norfolk. Other representations, with arrows, may be seen at: North Walsham, Saxlingham, Denton, Barton Turf, Trimingham, Brooke, Colney, all in Norfolk; and Whaddon in Cambs. At Padbury, Bucks., a wall painting depicts the wolf with St. Edmund's head; at Lakenheath, Suffolk and at Pickering, Yorks., there are wall paintings of the saint with arrows.

ST. EDMUND RICH (1170-1240)   16th November

Born at Abingdon he became a scholar and later Archbishop of Canterbury. At Oxford one of his students was Richard of Chichester (see later). Edmund died, exhausted by the demands of his office, at Burgundy and was canonised in 1247. St. Edmund's College, near Standon, Herts., is a Roman Catholic School named after him.

KING EDWARD II (d. 1327)

Edward was murdered at Berkeley, Glos. and his tomb, in Gloucester Cathedral, became a place of pilgrimage. As he was not canonized he is an unofficial "saint".

ST. EDWARD THE CONFESSOR (c. 1002-1066)
                                         13th October

Edward the Confessor, King of England, had a humility and love for his subjects that was shown in many ways. Under his direction the famous Abbey of St. Peter, Westminster was built. His shrine still stands within its walls.

His shield shows a cross surrounded by five martlets

14

(heraldic swallows). The background of the shield is blue. The cross and the martlets are gold.

Other emblems which remind us of his kingship are a sceptre and a ring. His effigy may be seen at Westminster and Exeter Cathedral.

ST. EDWARD OF CORFE (c. 963-978)   18th March
This Saxon boy king was murdered at his stepmother's instigation in Corfe Castle, Dorset. (Is this why literature is festooned with wicked stepmothers?) His shrine was set up in Shaftesbury Abbey by St. Dunstan. His emblems are a dagger and cup, dagger and sceptre, and a short sword. Edward's effigy appears on the west front at Wells Cathedral.

ST. EGWIN (7th Cent.)   30th December
A bishop of Worcester and founder of Evesham Abbey. Two dedications.

ST. ERKENWALD (7th Cent.)   13th May
Erkenwald founded the abbeys at Barking and Chertsey. St. Ethelberga, his sister, was the first abbess at the latter house. He became bishop of London and was buried in St. Paul's. There is one church dedicated to his sister.

ST. ETHELBERT (d. 616)   25th February
The Saxon King Ethelbert of Kent met Augustine on the Isle of Thanet in 597. His effigy may be seen at Wells Cathedral. There are sixteen churches dedicated to him; at Stanway, Essex the dedication is to St. Albright, an alternative form of his name.

ST. ETHELDREDA (AUDREY) (d. 679)   17th October
Etheldreda, the daughter of a Christian prince, was the founder of the monastery at Ely and became its first abbess.

From another form of her name we get the word tawdry which means cheap finery. St. Audrey's lace used to be sold at the fair held on her feast day at Ely.

She is often shown crowned, holding a crozier and a book as at Norbury, Derbys. (window) and Upton, Norfolk (rood-screen). Twelve dedications.

ST. ETHELWOLD (905-984)   1st August
Ethelwold was a monk at Glastonbury who became Abbot of Abingdon and later Bishop of Winchester. He was a scholar, musician and mathematician. One church is dedicated to him.

15

ST. FAITH (3rd Cent.)   6th October
St. Faith was martyred in France in the third century.
The sword and the grid-iron bear witness to her suffering for
her faith, and she is shown on a brass at St. Lawrence's,
Norwich.

ST. FELIX (d. 648)   8th March
He was a bishop from Burgundy sent to preach the gospel
in East Anglia. His name survives in Felixstowe. It is easy to
confuse him with the other sixty saints of the same name! There
are six churches dedicated to him.

ST. FRIDESWIDE (d. 735)   19th October
Frideswide was a princess who became a nun and founded a
nunnery on the site of the present Christ Church, Oxford.
Patron of the City and University, she appears on the Diocesan
Arms with two demi-maidens. Her holy well at Osney is still
visited by many people each year. Henry VIII visited the well
with Catherine of Aragon. Frideswide is shown in the east
window at Osney. Dedications are at Frilsham, Berks.; Osney,
Oxford and Water Eaton, Bucks.

ST. GEORGE (d. c. 303)   23rd April
George is the patron saint of England. He was born of
Christian parents at Cappadocia. His father suffered a martyr's
death and his mother fled with him to Israel. He was tortured
by Diocletian and among the horrors he is said to have
endured are: running in red hot iron shoes, being broken
on a spiked wheel, immersed in quick-lime, and bound beneath
a heavy stone. In Christian art he usually appears in conflict
with the legendary dragon. His white banner with its red
cross forms the basis of the Union Jack. Examples may be
seen at: Hempstead (roodscreen), Ranworth (parclose screen)
and Filby (roodscreen), all in Norfolk. At Thorpe Arnold,
Leics. St. George appears engraved on the Norman font
attacking two dragons. See also page 30.

ST. GILBERT OF SEMPRINGHAM (1083-1189)
                                               4th February
Gilbert was the founder of the only English Order—at
Sempringham, Lincs. The canons followed the Augustine rule
and the nuns observed the Cistercian vows. There were twenty-
six Gilbertine houses and although canons and nuns had sep-
arate cloisters they worshipped together in one church. At the
Dissolution those at Sempringham, St. Catherine's, Lincoln
and Chicksands, Beds. ranked as great houses. He is shown on
the roodscreen at Alphington, Devon.

ST. GILES (8th Cent.) 1st September

St. Giles was a Greek of noble birth. He was born in Athens in the 8th century, and was brought up as a Christian.

One story about St. Giles tells how he saved some sailors, in peril of being dashed upon the rocks, by his prayers. The sailors were so thankful that they offered him a passage in their ship. Giles travelled to France.

Eventually Giles went into the stony wastes of southern France to live as a hermit. One day he found a hind drinking at a well among the rocks. Giles made friends with the animal and shared his lonely dwelling with her. On one occasion the king's huntsmen chased the hind. When Giles saw her in peril he prayed for her safety, and the hounds stopped in their tracks and turned away. When the king heard of these strange events he decided to investigate. Setting out with his soldiers he came upon St. Giles's retreat. A soldier loosed an arrow into the thicket which surrounded Giles's hut in the hope of disturbing the hind. The shaft struck the seated figure of Giles in the chest. Hearing the old man cry out the king's party entered the hollow to find the wounded hermit with the hind sheltering behind him. The king was filled with remorse and offered Giles many treasures to compensate for his wound. The saint refused worldly wealth, but accepted land from the king so that he could build a monastery. This was soon completed and he became its first abbot.

St. Giles was a popular saint in mediaeval times. Important trading fairs were held and took place on his feast day in Winchester and Oxford. Some school children near Oxford still enjoy an extra day's holiday each year to attend the traditional St. Giles's fair which takes place in the street named after him.

St. Giles is shown on the font of Norwich Cathedral with the hind leaping up to him. He is often depicted with the arrow piercing his chest. The hind and the arrow are his distinctive emblems.

ST. GOVAN

This Celtic local saint has been partly ignored by hagiologists—but geography is on his side and the Pembrokeshire promontory, south of Bosherston, bears his name. Govan's chapel and well are set among precipitous cliffs. Even in the last century a number of cures were recorded at the well. The small chamber which is traditionally St. Govan's original cell may still be seen near the stone altar. Although the chapel is small it closes the pass between the rock strewn cove and the cliff top. Long ago in its open belfry there hung a silver bell. One summer evening, so the legend says, a group of men sailed into the cove to steal the bell. It was taken down and placed in their boat, but as soon as they left the shore a violent storm arose and the thieves perished. The bell was borne away miraculously and entombed in a massive stone at the brink of the well. When the stone is struck its silver tones are supposed to echo within.

ST. GUTHLAC (7th Cent.)   11th April

Guthlac was a fierce Mercian warrior who was converted overnight by a dream. He entered the monastery at Repton and two years or so later he was given permission to depart to find a hermitage. The loneliest and, then, most inhospitable part of England gave shelter to the pious Guthlac; and on St. Bartholomew's day he was rowed through the swamps to Crowland (Croyland) which became his lifelong home and the site of an important abbey.

Many stories became attached to his name after his death. One day a servant was tempted to cut Guthlac's throat as he was shaving him. So great were the saint's powers of perception however that the servant's thoughts were exposed and he confessed. On another occasion, he rebuked some wayward ravens which had tormented him by stealing small things from the brethren and visitors, and they returned their plunder.

In Christian art Guthlac is shown putting devils to flight with a scourge in his hand; or with a whip and a serpent at his feet.

Crowland Abbey is still full of interest for the visitor. Above the west door of the ruined nave are carved scenes from the saint's life. They show (1) Tatwin the boatman bringing Guthlac to Crowland. Guthlac was given a sign to show him where to land and the sow under a willow tree with a litter of pigs is included in the carvings; (2) the saint's ordination; (3) Guthlac making the devil bring stone for the abbey; (4) Guthlac wrapped in a shroud; (5) the saint ascending. The site of Guthlac's cell is marked at the west end of the south aisle.

Scenes from Guthlac's life may also be found in the windows of the church at Market Deeping—not far away—which is one of the nine churches dedicated to him.

ST. HELEN (255-330)   18th August

St. Helen is credited with the finding of Our Lord's cross on Calvary. Two "of the worst liars in the middle ages", Geoffrey of Monmouth and Henry of Huntingdon, advanced the questionable traditions concerning her. Old King Cole of Colchester was supposed to have been her father but she was certainly not a native of these islands. Her emblem is a cross—and can be seen at Alphington, Devon; Stratton Strawless, Norfolk; and on the Seal of Colchester. A stained glass portrait of the saint appears in St. Helen's church, Abingdon, Oxon.

ST. HILDA OF WHITBY (614-680)   17th November
St. Hilda was abbess of Whitby. She was a contemporary of John of Beverley, Cademon the Poet and St. Aidan. Fifteen dedications.

ST. HUGH OF AVALON (Great Hugh) (1135-1200)
               17th November
Hugh was a wise and fearless bishop of Lincoln whose pet swan met him each time he returned to his palace. Emblem— a swan. Effigy—St. Mary's spire, Oxford. One dedication.

ST. HUGH OF LINCOLN (Little Hugh) (d. 1255)
                 27th July
Little Hugh was a child who was murdered and thrown into a well at Lincoln. The story appears in Chaucer's 'Prioress's Tale'. See also—St. William of Norwich.

ST. IVAN (YVO)   24th April
Ivan was a Persian bishop. His body was "discovered" at St. Ives, Cambs, in 1001 and this gave the town the name it now bears. The Cornish St. Ive and St. Ives may also derive from this name, but Dorset's St. Ives seems to come from an Old English word indicating ivy.

ST. JOHN (1st Cent.)   27th December
After the Crucifixion, John, the author of the fourth Gospel appears to have remained in Jerusalem. During the persecution of Domitian he was taken to Rome. Outside the Latin Gate he was immersed in a cauldron of boiling oil but suffered no harm, and was sent to work in the mines at Patmos.

Many symbols are associated with him but his principal emblem is the eagle and this device is frequently found on mediaeval memorial brasses. Hundreds of churches possess a lectern shaped in the form of an eagle and St. John must no doubt be credited with this traditional design. Other signs connected with him are: a cup with a serpent issuing from it— Worstead, Norfolk (roodscreen); Ranworth, Norfolk (roodscreen); a sword and a palm— N. Walsham, Norfolk (roodscreen); Trunch, Norfolk (roodscreen).

ST. JOHN THE BAPTIST (1st Cent.)   24th June

St. John the Baptist is a popular saint in England. The reference he makes (see John Ch. 1.) to Our Lord as "The Lamb of God" provides him with his symbol—a lamb. This emblem made him a popular saint among the wool merchants of the middle ages and many churches in the old wool producing areas are dedicated to him. The lamb emblem may be found at: Ranworth, Worstead and Attleborough, all in Norfolk. Five hundred dedications.

ST. JOHN OF BEVERLEY (640-721)   7th May

John was the Archbishop of York who consecrated Bede. His shrine lies in the Minster at Beverley which he founded. Seven dedications.

ST. JOHN FISHER (1468-1535)   4th May

John Fisher was chancellor of Cambridge. He would not subscribe to the annulment of Henry VIII's marriage with Catherine of Aragon and was executed on Tower Hill on 22nd June 1535. He is buried at All Hallows, Barking and was canonized in 1935. See also Sir Thomas More.

SIR JOHN SCHORNE (d. 1308)

An uncanonised saint, he was held in high esteem during the middle ages. He was renowned for his piety—his knees grew horny through constant prayer. At North Marston, Bucks., where he was Rector, he conjured the Devil into a boot—hence the origin of the jack in the box. Vast numbers of pilgrims visited his shrine and it was moved to St. George's, Windsor. John Schorne was a good saint to invoke "for the ague". He appears on rood screens at: Alphington and Wolborough in Devon; Gateley and Cawston in Norfolk. The preponderance of Boot inns in and around Buckinghamshire owes much to his reputation.

ST. JOSEPH OF ARIMATHEA (1st Cent.)   17th March

Joseph of Arimathea allowed Jesus's body to be laid in his own tomb. He came to England to preach the Gospel about 60 A.D. and brought with him the Holy Grail (the cup used at the Last Supper) and a staff cut from the thorn-bush from which our Lord's crown of thorns was made.

On Christmas morning Joseph visited Glastonbury and there left his staff implanted in the ground. It took root and grew into a tree. Each Christmas white blooms appear on the Holy Thorn in Glastonbury which is said to be an off-shoot of Joseph's original staff. Joseph later built a chapel of wattle and daub in Glastonbury. This was one of England's first churches. The chapel was burnt down during the twelfth century and later replaced by the Abbey, the ruins of which can be seen today.

A spray of Glastonbury Thorn is sent to the Queen each Christmas.

Joseph's emblems are a box of ointment or a budding staff.

ST. JUSTUS (d. 626)   10th November

Justus was the first Bishop of Rochester, Kent.

ST. KENELM (d. 819)   17th July

Traditionally he was murdered as a youth in the Clent Hills, Worcs., but according to some authorities he seems to have reached manhood. He was a member of the royal house of Mercia and his shrine was at Winchcombe Abbey, Glos. St. Kenelm's Well and chapel nearby mark the last resting place of the saint's body on its journey to Winchcombe. The spring is said to have appeared on this occasion. Other dedications are at: Alderley, Coln St. Dennis and Sapperton, Glos.; Clifton-on-Teme, Worcs.; Enstone and Minster Lovell, Oxon. St. Kenelm's effigy appears on the west front of Wells Cathedral, and on St. Kenelm's chapel.

ST. LAURENCE (d. 258)   10th August

Saint Laurence was Archdeacon of Rome during the third century. At this time the Christian Emperor Philip was assassinated by the conspirator Decius, who became the Emperor Decius Caesar. He at once tried to find Philip's treasure. When he discovered that Philip had given all his riches to the Church he became very angry.

Sixtus, Bishop of Rome, hearing of the Emperor's anger and fearing arrest instructed Laurence to dispose of all the treasure as soon as possible. Working during the night to avoid inquisitive eyes, Laurence distributed all the wealth entrusted to him. He was only just in time.

Bishop Sixtus was arrested and Decius demanded the treasure. Sixtus would not reveal his secret, and Decius arrested Laurence and ordered him to produce the Church's treasures within three days.

For three days and nights Laurence worked collecting together all the poor, blind and lame Christians in the city. On the third day he returned to the Emperor. "Here are the Church's treasures" he said, pointing to his followers. The enraged Decius commanded Laurence to sacrifice to the pagan gods. Laurence refused, and was brutally tortured, finally dying from being bound to a grid iron and slowly burned over a fire.

21

Christians remembered Laurence by using a grid iron as his emblem. Many churches in England are dedicated to this saint. Examples of his emblem may be found at Harpley, Norfolk ; Little Kimble and Winslow, Bucks. ; and in Balliol College Library, Oxford.

ST. LUKE (1st Cent.)   18th October

Saint Luke is an important saint in the Church's Calendar. He was the author of the Third Gospel and the Acts of the Apostles.

St. Luke has been represented in various ways in Christian art. In a sixteenth century primer he is shown painting a portrait of the Blessed Virgin Mary. His distinctive symbol, as an evangelist, is a winged ox. At East Ruston, Norfolk, he is shown with an ox lying near him. On the altarpiece of St. Catarina, Pisa, he is shown holding a book supported by such a beast. At Wells Cathedral an interesting mediaeval clock is decorated with the symbols of the four evangelists.

ST. MARK (1st Cent.)   25th April

Mark wrote the second Gospel. Tradition claims that he was eventually put to death in Egypt by being dragged through the streets by the neck. He was buried in Alexandria, but in 815 Venetian merchants carried his relics to Italy, and a suitable church dedicated to him was eventually built to shelter his mortal remains. He has been represented in art being dragged by the neck, being strangled, and seated beneath a fig tree. At East Ruston, Norfolk, he is shown on the rood-screen with a lion by his side, and the winged lion is his most widely used symbol.

ST. MARTIN (4th Cent.)   11th October

St. Martin is remembered for giving half his cloak to a poor beggar. At St. Martin's, Fenny Stratford, Bucks, special fireworks known as Fenny Poppers are set off by the church-wardens on his feast day. See also page 34.

ST. MATTHEW (1st Cent.)   21st September

When Matthew, a Jew and the hated collector of Roman taxes, was called by Jesus to become an apostle many people must have been shocked. The Gospels tell how angry the Pharisees were to learn that Our Lord had befriended a traitor to his own people.

Early Christians believed that Matthew was the author of the first Gospel which bears his name ; but modern biblical scholars feel that the real author was probably another Jew who lived late in the first century A.D.

Matthew is said to have suffered martyrdom. One story records that he was slain by the sword for opposing a king who wished to marry an unwilling princess.

Matthew's usual symbol, an angel, is suggested by the first chapter of the Gospel attributed to him. This records the angel's visit to Joseph. Other emblems associated with the Apostle are a money bag (tax collector) and a sword (martyrdom).

Matthew's traditional symbol may be found engraved on mediaeval memorial brasses in many churches: St. Cross, Winchester, Hants. (1382); Higham Ferrers, Northants (1400); Christ Church, Oxford (1557) and West Hanney, Berks. (1557).

ST. MATTHIAS (1st Cent.) 24th February

Matthias was chosen, after Ascension Day, by the eleven remaining Apostles to replace the traitor Judas Iscariot.

The painting by the German artist, Hans Baldung, in Freiburg Minster, shows Matthias holding an ornate halberd. An English example may be found at Fairford, Gloucester.

Matthias has given his name to twenty English churches. At the College of St. Matthias, Fishponds, Bristol, his feast day is an event of special importance.

THE BLESSED VIRGIN MARY Principal Feast 15th August

Mary, mother of Our Lord, is the most venerated of the saints—she has 2,335 English dedications. Pilgrims still visit the shrine of Our Lady at Little Walsingham, Norfolk. Her principal emblem is the lily.

ST. MELLITUS (d. 624) 24th April

Mellitus was the first Bishop of London.

ST. MICHAEL ARCHANGEL 29th September

Over six hundred churches are dedicated to St. Michael, and representations of him may be found in many more: Bartlow, Cambs.; Broughton and Little Hampden, Bucks.; Swalcliffe, Oxon.; Lew Trenchard, Devon. The outstanding modern work depicting him is at Coventry Cathedral—a bronze by Epstein.

ST. NICHOLAS (4th Cent.) 6th December

St. Nicholas, the son of a rich nobleman, was Bishop of Myra, Asia Minor, during the early part of the fourth century. Although many legends concerning his acts have been handed down to us, very little is known about his life and work as a bishop.

Nicholas is best remembered for his kindness to an impoverished nobleman and his three daughters. The nobleman, unable to pay the necessary dowries which would allow his daughters to marry men of high rank, was tempted to sell them into slavery. Nicholas is said to have saved the young girls by secretly providing them with dowries. One night he made his way to the nobleman's house and, while the household was asleep, cast three heavy bags of gold through an open window. The nobleman was overjoyed at his good fortune and his daughters were saved.

The story of the three bags of gold forms the basis of the saint's symbol—three golden balls. Pawnbrokers adopted the emblem, and used it as a trade sign. Some examples are still in use today.

Another legend records how Nicholas saved sailors in peril and makes him the patron of seafarers. It may be for this reason that so many of the nearly four hundred English churches dedicated to him are situated on the coast at places as far apart as Whitehaven, Cumbria and Great Yarmouth in Norfolk.

As the patron saint of children St. Nicholas (Santa Claus) is of course traditionally responsible for filling the Christmas stocking. In some European countries, like Holland, children receive Santa Claus' presents on his feast day, 6th December. There is a good sixteenth century window at Hillesden, Bucks., showing scenes from his life. See also page 30.

ST. OSMUND (d. 1099)   4th December

Osmund was a chaplain and later became Bishop of Sarum. He was the author of the Sarum Use which so influenced the development of the English liturgical pattern. His body was translated to the new cathedral from Old Sarum in 1457. Osmund's shrine is in Salisbury Cathedral.

ST. OSWALD, King of Northumbria (604-642)   9th August

Oswald was slain by the heathen Penda at Oswestry (St. Oswald's Tree). His dismembered body was nailed to a tree. Oswald's hand was enshrined at Bamburgh Castle, and his head was placed in Cuthbert's tomb at Durham. Sixty-seven churches are dedicated to him and many are situated near a well or spring. At St. Oswald's, Kirkoswald, Cumb. a spring emerges from the west wall. His emblem is a sceptre and a cross.

ST. OSWALD OF WORCESTER (d. 992)   28th February

Oswald was St. Dunstan's successor to the See of Worcester. He later became Archbishop of York and held both dioceses together. The important monastery at Ramsey, Cambs, was founded by him. His effigy appears on the west front at Wells Cathedral.

ST. OSWIN (d. 651)   **20th August**

Oswin was a cousin of King Oswald (see above). Another relation, King Oswy, plotted his death which took place at Gilling, Yorks. His emblems are a spear (Delamare brass, St. Albans) and a spear and sceptre (seal of Tynemouth Priory).

ST. OSYTH, SITHA (7th Cent.)   **7th October**

Osyth was an East Saxon queen who gave her name to the Essex village where her nunnery stands. Her emblems are two keys and three loaves; or a rosary, bag and keys. She is shown at Ashton, Devon (rood); Mells, Som. (window); St. Sidwell's Exeter (carving). Four dedications.

ST. PANCRAS (d. 304)   **12th May**

He was a Roman martyr whose name was introduced into England by St. Augustine. Ten churches bear the name of Pancras but some seem to be dedicated to Pancras of Taormina—of Greek origin. The name is best known in England as the London railway terminus.

Emblems—sword and stone in his hand; youth armed holding a book and palm with a Saracen under his feet (Cowfold, Sussex—memorial brass of Prior Nelond).

ST. PAULINUS (d. 644)   **10th October**

Paulinus was the first bishop of York. Five English churches are dedicated to him.

ST. PAUL (1st Cent.)   **25th January**

St. Paul—Apostle to the Gentiles—was martyred at Rome. He is a popular saint in England with about three hundred and twenty six dedications. Wren's cathedral in London is named after him and Paul's emblem—a sword—is shown on the city arms. There is a good twelfth century painting of Paul in Canterbury Cathedral. Another interesting painting of him can be found at Thornham Parva, Suffolk.

ST. PETER (1st Cent.)   **29th June**

St. Peter (Simon Peter—the fisherman) has been called the Prince of the Apostles. After the Ascension Peter became the leader of the early Church. He was the first to perform a miracle in Our Lord's name (Act 3; 1-10). His name means 'rock'.

St. Matthew's Gospel (16:19) records how Jesus said to him "I will give you the keys of the kingdom of heaven". It is from this saying that Peter's emblem of crossed keys originates. He ended his life in Rome as its first bishop. According to tradition he was crucified upside down.

York Cathedral is dedicated to him, and the crossed keys appear on the diocesan arms. St. Peter has given his name to the churches at: Peterchurch, Hereford, Petersfield, Hants., Petersham, Surrey, Petersmarland, Devon; and Peterstow, Hereford. The following churches, which are also dedicated to him, contain examples of his emblem: Cassington, Oxon.— east window; Crostwick, Norfolk—font; Melton Mowbray, Leics., Ringland, Norfolk—roodscreen; Thornham Parva, Suffolk; Westminster Abbey—mural. Over a thousand churches are dedicated to him, and the church at Bottesford, Humberside, is dedicated to St. Peter's Chains.

ST. RICHARD OF CHICHESTER (1197-1253)   3rd April

Richard was born at Droitwich, Worcestershire. His father was a hard working yeoman. Both Richard's parents died while he was still a minor and by the time he and his brother became of age the substance of the estate had been dissipated. After working to restore the estate's former prosperity, he went to Oxford where he spent his student days in a state of near poverty. Richard's long years of manual labour proved to be a great help to him in later years and his considerable stature as a scholar was tempered by a real and sympathetic understanding of the countryman's ways.

From Oxford Richard went to Bologna for seven years and on his return he became Chancellor of Oxford. Later he became Chancellor of Canterbury. When his friend Edmund Rich died Richard went to Orleans and while he was there he became a priest. He returned to England to become the parish priest at Deal. Once again he became Chancellor of Canterbury—under Boniface of Savoy.

Henry III was then King of England and he, having disagreed with the Pope, was in conflict with the Church. Henry wished to appoint a favourite to the vacant See of Chichester. As the bishops could not accept the candidate's suitability Henry confiscated all the See's temporal assets. When Richard was made bishop he had no palace to live in, and he made his home at Tarring Neville—not far from the coast near Newhaven. Leo Sherley-Price in *Saints of England* (1936) notes that there still existed at that time an orchard of figs at Tarring "whose trees are descendants of those which Richard tended". After eight years as bishop this humble scholar—who often went on foot about his diocese and lived a life of austerity and simplicity—died at Dover. On the day before his death in 1253 he consecrated a chapel at Dover to his old friend St. Edmund Rich.

Richard was buried at Chichester and his shrine soon became a place of pilgrimage—he was canonized by Pope Urban IV in 1262 (on St. Vincent's Day).

St. Richard is sometimes represented ploughing: sometimes with a chalice at his feet or kneeling before one. With the development of heraldry in the middle ages many saints had shields of arms attributed to them. Richard's arms show a silver cross between four silver cups on a red shield. These arms may still be seen in a window in Chichester cathedral.

ST. RICHARD WHITING (d. 1539)   1st December
Richard was the last Abbot of Glastonbury. He refused to acknowledge Henry VIII as supreme head of the English Church, was sent to the Tower, and was later hanged and quartered with two companions, on Glastonbury Tor.

ROBERT OF KNARESBOROUGH (date uncertain)
Robert is an unofficial saint. He was a hermit and his chapel remains at Knaresborough.

STS. SIMON AND JUDE (1st Cent.)   28th October
Simon and Jude were brothers of James the Less and Joseph Barsabas. They were martyred: Simon is supposed to have been sawn in half, and his brother Jude slain with a halberd.

Simon's emblem is a saw (Exeter Cathedral). He is the patron saint of woodcutters. Other symbols associated with him are fishes (Ranworth and Aylsham, Norfolk), an oar (Southwold, Suffolk, and Stalham, Norfolk) and a fuller's bat (Cawston, Norfolk).

St. Jude (Thaddeus) may be identified by the following: a boat in his hand (N. Walsham, Norfolk), a boathook, a carpenter's square (Weston Longville, Norfolk), a fuller's bat in his hand, carrying loaves or fish (Fairford, Glos.), a club (Melbury Bubb, Dorset), carrying an inverted cross, a halberd.

ST. STEPHEN (1st Cent.)   26th December
St. Stephen was a follower of Our Lord's teaching, and was made a deacon by the Apostles after the Ascension. In Jerusalem he performed various miracles. His vigorous preaching caused some of his opponents to denounce him to the Sanhedrin, the highest Jewish Court of Justice. He was brought before the court. His brilliant speech in his own defence, which is recorded in the seventh chapter of the Acts of the Apostles, so enraged the accusers that they fell upon him and cast him out of the city. He was stoned to death.

Stephen was a popular saint during the middle ages. There are some one hundred and twenty-five English churches dedicated to him. Three Cornish villages also commemorate his name: St. Stephen-by-Launceston, St. Stephen-by-Saltash, and St. Stephen-in-Brannel.

In Christian art he is usually represented as a deacon. His distinctive emblems are stones and a book.

ST. SWITHIN (800-862) 15th July

St. Swithin was Bishop of Winchester. The tradition concerning the forty days of rain arose when the Heavens shed their tears as his body was translated from its humble grave to a place of honour within the cathedral in 971.

ST. THEODORE OF TARSUS (620-690) 19th September

He was Archbishop of Canterbury and a native of St. Paul's home town. Theodore was a contemporary of Bede, Cuthbert, John of Beverley and Wilfrid.

ST. THOMAS à BECKET (1118-1170) 29th December

Thomas à Becket was Archbishop of Canterbury. He was slain on 29th December 1170 in his own cathedral—on the choir steps—at the hands of de Moreville, le Breton, de Tracy and Fitzurse, four knights of Henry II. His shrine became, in mediaeval days, the principal place of pilgrimage in England. To it came the pilgrims of Chaucer's *Canterbury Tales*. He is shown in a window at St. Mary's, Warwick.

ST. THOMAS OF HEREFORD (1218-1282) 3rd October

St. Thomas was a scholar who was made Chancellor of England by King Henry III in 1265. As a bishop he is specially remembered for his care of the poor. He died returning from a visit to Rome, and was buried in his cathedral at Hereford. During the middle ages many pilgrims visited his shrine.

His own shield of arms is still used by the Bishop of Hereford. This shows three gold leopards' faces upside down each with a lily held in the mouth, on a red background.

ST. THOMAS MORE (1478-1535) 4th May/9th July

Thomas More was Lord Chancellor of England. After refusing to assent to the Acts of Supremacy and Succession he was tried and executed on Tower Hill. In 1935 he was formally canonized. More was the author of *Utopia*. Robert Bolt's play *A Man for All Seasons* reveals the tensions of More's life and times. He is now included in the new Roman Calendar. See page 30.

ST. UNCUMBER (Wilgeforte) 20th July

A legendary saint, from Portugal, she prayed for a beard to

help her to preserve her vows of virginity. Her effigy is in Henry VII's Chapel, Westminster. She is also shown at Worstead, Norfolk (rood-screen).

ST. VINCENT (d.c. 303)   22nd January
St. Vincent was the first Spanish martyr. He was Archdeacon of Saragossa early in the fourth century.

In 303 the Emperor Diocletian ordered the seizure of all Christian clergy throughout the Roman Empire. Vincent was sent to prison. His brilliant speech in defence of his faith so enraged the local governor, Dacianus, that he ordered Vincent's execution.

Vincent's emblems—an iron hook and spiked grid iron—recall the terrible tortures he suffered. Finally a millstone was tied about his neck and he was drowned.

The arms of the city of Lisbon contain a boat with ravens perched on the prow and stern. These commemorate the legend that St. Vincent's body, cast adrift in an open boat, was guarded by ravens as it drifted from Lisbon to the Cape which bears his name.

Only five English churches are named in his memory.

ST. WERBERGA (d. 699)   3rd February
Werberga was a Mercian princess who took the veil. Her shrine was built in Chester Cathedral, and on a misericord (in the Choir) the enchanting legend of the convent geese is portrayed. Twelve dedications.

ST. WILFRID (634-709)   12th October
Wilfred was a Bishop of York and an active evangelist. His unbending convictions brought him into conflict with both the king and the Archbishop of Canterbury. He was nevertheless an outstanding figure of his age. In art he is usually shown baptising pagans. He is a popular saint with forty-eight dedications. St. Wilfrid's Chair—the bishop's throne—at Hexham was once the Sanctuary Seat.

ST. WILLIAM OF YORK (d. 1154)   8th June
William was Archbishop of York and miracles attributed to him are shown in the windows of the Minster.

ST. WILLIAM OF NORWICH (d. 1144)   26th March
William was a boy whose mutilated body was left in a wood outside Norwich. This murder was unjustly attributed to the Jews of the city. He is shown on the roodscreen at Worstead and Loddon, Norfolk. See also—Little Hugh of Lincoln.

ST. WULFSTAN (1007-1095) 19th January

Wulfstan was Bishop of Worcester and a vigorous opponent of the slave trade that operated between Bristol and Ireland. He is shown in a window at the Priory Church, Gt. Malvern, Worcs.

PASCHALIS MYSTERII

Since the dawn of man's perception he has found comfort in the symbols created to inspire or guide his ideals. Several millennia ago Avebury and Stonehenge were fashioned for such a purpose and so—less distant in time—was Uffington's White Horse. The mediaeval mind embraced the notion of sainthood with similar intent and it remained unsullied until Pope Paul VI pronounced his *Paschalis Mysterii* in May 1969 and numerous saints had to hand in their haloes! Among those whose names have been removed from the new Roman calendar—as their existence is now questioned—are St. Barbara, St. Catherine of Alexandria and St. Christopher. The Scottish tradition that St. Christopher was a native named Nial whose name was changed on canonization seems to have been discounted. In contrast the new calendar retains Sts. Michael, Gabriel and Raphael—Angels! Motorists now presumably dangle impotent medallions from their key-rings; and golfers—bereft of St. Barbara's skill with lightning—risk Thor's wrath every time they trundle their clubs across the links.

St. George too has suffered and his feast becomes optional. His relegation has brought forth a number of suggestions for his replacement as England's Patron Saint by Alban, Augustine, Edmund or Swithin. Another casualty is St. Nicholas (Santa Claus) but there is staunch support for his cause from those with a vested interest in his alleged beneficence.

Paschalis Mysterii poses a few problems. Logic seems to demand that churches' dedicated to non-saints should be renamed—but this is not to be. Anglicans will doubtless be quick to uphold Article XXXVII and assert that "The Bishop of Rome hath no jurisdiction in this realm of England".

The saints have little temporal redress. Spiritual redundancy does not seem to qualify for even an honorary halo.

In the days long before our present weather forecasters countrymen had worked out their own explanations of the climate. Many of these ideas, and some of them may go back to pre-Christian times, became attached to saints. There are too many such sayings and beliefs to include them all, but a selection of the more interesting ones is arranged below:

JANUARY

2nd St. Macarius of Alexandria: This day sheweth the nature and state of September. (Diall of Daies).

14th St. Hilary: The coldest day of the year. (Yorkshire).

17th St. Antony the Hermit: St. Antony brings ice or breaks it.
St. Antony makes bridges, and St. Paul (Jan. 25) breaks them.

25th Conversion of St. Paul:
If the sun shines on this day, it betokens a good year; if it rain or snow, indifferent; if misty, it predicts a great dearth; if it thunder, great winds and death of people that year. (Book of knowledge).
If it be a fair day, it will be a pleasant year. If it be windy, there will be wars: If it be cloudy, it foreshadows the plague. (Diall of Daies).

FEBRUARY

2nd Purification of the Blessed Virgin Mary (Candlemas):
If Candlemas-day be fair and bright,
Winter will have another flight:
But if it be dark with clouds and rain,
Winter is gone and won't come again.
If Candlemas-day be fine and clear,
Corn and fruit will then be dear.
If the wind's in the east on Candlemas Day
It's sure to stay to the second of May.

24th St. Matthie sends sap into the tree. St. Matthias sows both leaf and grass.

MARCH

1st St. David:
Upon St. David's day
Put oats and barley in the clay.

2nd St. Chad:
> David and Chad
> Sow peas, good or bad.

3rd St. Winnold:
> First comes David, then comes Chad,
> And then comes Winnold, as though he were mad.

(An allusion to the boisterous winds often found at this time.)

21st St. Benedict: Sow thy peas or keep them in the rick.

25th Annunciation of the Blessed Virgin Mary: St. Mary blows out the candle, St. Michael (Sept. 29) lights it again.

APRIL

6th Old Lady Day:
> On Lady-day the latter
> The cold comes over the water.

25th St. Mark: To smell of April and May, Black Cross Day. (St. Mark's day was so called from the black covers of the crosses and relics in the processions of the Great Litany—instituted by St. Gregory.)

MAY

12th St. Pancras: There is a belief on the Continent that very cold weather, a second winter, may be expected in the middle of May.

25th St. Urban: If it rains on Urban's day every ear of corn loses a grain.

26th St. Philip of Neri: If it rains on St. Philip's day, the poor man has no need to beg of the rich.

JUNE

8th St. Medard: On St. Medard's day it rains six weeks before or six weeks after.
> St. Medard's drops drop for forty days.

9th St. Faustus: St. Faustus said to St. Medard: "Barnabas and Vitus are my neighbours, and together we will give the country folk a good washing till Frederick the Hollander (July 18) comes and closes the doors of heaven".

11th St. Barnabas:
> On St. Barnabas
> Put the scythe to the grass.
> Barnaby bright
> The longest day and the shortest night.

15th St. Vitus:
> If St. Vitus's day be rainy weather,
> It will rain for thirty days together.

24th   St. John the Baptist: If Midsummer Day be near so little rainy, the hazel and walnut will be scarce; corn smitten in many places: but apples pears and plums will not be hurt.   (Shepherd's Kalendar)

> Midsummer rain
> Spoils hay and grain.
> Cut your thistles before St. John
> You will have two instead of one.

JULY

1st   St. Calais:

> If the first of July be rainy weather,
> 'Twill rain more or less for four weeks together.

13th   St. Margaret puts the sickle to the corn.

15th   St. Swithin:

> If St. Swithin weeps the proverb says,
> The weather will be foul for forty days.
>
>   (Country Almanac, 1675)
>
> St. Swithin's day if thou be fair,
> 'Twill rain for forty days nae mair:
> St. Swithin's day, if thou dost rain,
> For forty days it will remain.

If it rains on this day St. Swithin is said to be christening the apples.

    The old English traditions concerning St. Swithin have been questioned in recent times. Some authorities have suggested that they really originated in the pagan era and concerned the alleged prophetic character of certain days at about this time of year.

22nd   St. Mary Magdalene: On St. Mary Magdalene's day the nuts are full.

25th   St. James the Great: If it be so that the sun shine on St. James his day, it is a token of cold weather: but if it rain thereon it is a token of warm and moist weather.   (The Husbandman's Practice)

AUGUST

1st   St. Peter ad vincula: After Lammas, corn ripens as much by night as by day—because of the heavy night dews.

10th   St. Laurence: If it rain on St. Laurence, it is rather late but still in time.

15th   Assumption of Blessed Virgin Mary: If the sun do shine on the 15th August that is a good token, and especially for wind.   (The Husbandman's Practice)

28th   St. Augustine: On St. Augustine's day darn any clothes —in preparation for winter.

SEPTEMBER

29th St. Michael: If Michaelmas day be fine, the sun will shine much in the winter, though the wind at north east will frequently reign long and be sharp and nipping. (Shepherd's Kalendar)

> At Michaelmas time or a little before,
> Half an apple goes to the core:
> At Christmas time or a little after,
> A crab in the hedge and thanks to the grafter.

If thou wilt see and know how it will go next year, then take heed of the oak-apples about St. Michael's day, for by them you shall know how it shall be: If the Apples of the oak-tree when they be cut be within full of spiders, then followeth a naughty year; if the Apples have within them Flies, that betokens a meetly good year; if they have Maggots in them, then followeth a good year; if there be nothing in them, then followeth a great Dearth; if the Apples be many, and early ripe, so shall it be an early Winter, and very much snow shall be afore Christmas, and after that it shall be cold, if the inner part or kernel be fair and clear, then shall the Summer be fair, and Corn good also; but if they be very moist, then shall the Summer be moist; if they be lean, then shall there be a hot and dry Summer. (The Husbandman's Practice)

So many days old the moon is on Michaelmas day, so many floods after.

OCTOBER

In Lombardy the peasants expect a few fine days towards the middle of the month which they call St. Teresa's summer—her feast is on 15th Oct. All over Europe the warm weather which may occur at this time is given a similar name. Thus: the summer of St. Gall (16th), Germany; St. Martin's summer (11th) England; St. Bridget's summer (8th), Sweden; the summer of St. Wenceslas (Sept. 28), Bohemia; St. Luke's little summer (18th) England.

18th At St. Luke's day kill your pigs and bung up your barrels. (Spain)

Up to St. Luke's day put your hands where you like; after it keep them in your pockets.

28th Sts. Simon and Jude: Considered by many to be the first day of winter.

On St. Simon's day we throw the sickle away.

NOVEMBER

1st All Saints: All Saints day brings the second summer. All Saints summer lasts three hours, three days, or three weeks.

Other proverbs remind us of the approaching cold— At All Saints take muff and gloves.

On All Saints day, cut off some bark from a beech tree, and after that, a chip or a piece of wood; cut it: if it be dry, then the ensuing winter will be dry, but pretty warm and temperate, if moist, a wet winter.

(Shepherd's Kalendar)

30th St. Andrew: On St. Andrew's day, the night is twice as long as day.

DECEMBER

13th St. Lucy: In the old calendar this was the shortest day —Lucy light, the shortest day and the longest night.

21st St. Thomas: St. Thomas grey, the longest night and the shortest day.

Look at the weathercock on St. Thomas's day at 12 o'clock, and see which way the wind is; there it will stick for the next three months.

28th Innocents' Day: If it be lowering or wet on Childermas Day, it threatens scarcity and mortality among the weaker sort of young people; but if the day be very fair, it promises plenty. (Shepherd's Kalendar)

St. Aebba	St. Abbs, St. Abb's Head, Berwick.
St. Agnes	St. Agnes, St. Agnes Head, Cornwall.
St. Alban	St. Albans, Herts.: St. Alban's/Aldhelm's Head, Dorset.
St. Alun	St. Allen, Cornwall.
St. Andrew	St. Andrews, St. Andrews Bay, Fife: St. Andrews Major, Glam.
St. Anne	St. Anne, Alderney, C.I.: St. Anne's, Lancs.: St. Ann's, Dumf.: St. Ann's Chapel, Cornwall: St. Ann's Head, Pemb.: St. Ann's Hill, Cork.
St. Anthony	St. Anthony (in Roseland; in Meneage) Cornwall: Penzance (Holy/Saint's Headland/Cape)—attributed to St. Anthony by I. Taylor in *Words & Places*.
St. Arvan	St. Arvans, Mon.
St. Asaph	St. Asaph, Flints.
St. Athan	St. Athan, Glam.
St. Aubin	St. Aubin, St. Aubin's Bay, Jersey, C.I.
St. Austell	St. Austell, St. Austell Bay, Cornwall.
St. Baldred	St. Baldred's Boat, St. Baldred's Cradle, E. Lothian.
St. Bar	Kilbar, Isle of Barra, Hebrides.
St. Beya	St. Bees, St. Bees Head, Cumb—a virgin mentioned by Bede.
St. Bernard	St. Bernard, Wilts.
St. Blaise	St. Blazey, Cornwall.
St. Boswell	St. Boswells, Roxb.
St. Botolph	Botolph Claydon, Bucks. Boston (Botolph's Stone) Lincs.
St. Breock	St. Breock Downs, Corn.
St. Breward	St. Breward, Corn.
St. Briavel	St. Briavel, Glos.
St. Bride (Bridget)	St. Brides, St. Brides Bay, Pembs: St. Brides Major, Glam: St. Brides-super-Ely, Glam: St. Brides Wentlooge, Mon: Kilbride, Point Skye: Kilbride Bay, ·Argyll. Christopher Wren's church of St. Bride, Fleet St., London has a spire shaped like the tiers of a wedding cake.
St. Brynach	Llanfrynach, Brecknock.
St. Budoc	St. Budeaux, Devon.
St. Buryan	St. Buryan, Corn.

St. Cadoc	Llangattock, Brecknock and Mon; Cadoxton, Glam.
St. Caio	St. Kew, Corn.
St. Carannog	Crantock, Card.
St. Catherine	St. Catherine, Argyll: St. Catherine's Dub, A'deen: St. Catherine's Point, I.O.W.: St. Catherine's Hill, Winchester, Hants.
St. Celert	Beddgelert, Caerns. A 5th century Welsh saint. The Church at Llangeler, Çarms, is dedicated to him.
St. Ciarran	Kilkiaran, Islay:. Kilkerran, Ayr/Connemara.
St. Cleer	St. Clears, Carm: St. Cleer, Corn.
St. Clement	St. Clement, St. Clement's Isle, Corn.
St. Clether	St. Clether, Corn.
St. Colmac	St. Colmac, Isle of Bute.
St. Colme	St. Colme House, Fife.
St. Columba	St. Columkille's Oratory, Donegal: St. Columb Major/St. Columb Minor, St. Columb Road, Corn: Incolm Hill (Iona). The Apostle of the Picts who is said to have founded a hundred monasteries in Ireland and Scotland.
St. Collen	Llangollen. Denb. (A Roman soldier who became abbot of Glastonbury.)
St. Combs	St. Combs, A'deen.
St. Curig	Capel Curig, Caerns.
St. Cybi	Llangybi, Card/Mon: Caergybi, Anglesey.
St. Cyri	St. Cyrus, Kinc.
St. David	St. Davids, Fife/Pemb/Perths: St. David's Head, Palace, Pemb.
St. Day	St. Day, Corn.
St. Dalua	Killaloe, Clare.
St. Decuman	St. Decumans, Som. (A Welsh hermit who died at Dunster.)
St. Denis	St. Dennis, Corn: St. Denys, Hants.
St. Dinebo	Llandinabo, Heref.
St. Dogmaels	St. Dogwells, Pemb.
St. Dominic	St. Dominick, Corn.
St. Doulagh	St. Doulagh's Church, Dublin.
St. Dunwyd	St. Donats, Glam.
St. Dyfrig	St. Devereux, Heref.
St. Edith	St. Edith's Marsh, Wilts.
St. Edmund	Bury St. Edmunds. Suff.
St. Endellion	St. Endellion, Corn.

St. Enoder	St. Enoder, Corn.
St. Ercus	St. Erth, Corn. (A bishop of Slane, Ireland).
St. Erme	St. Erme, Corn.
St. Ervan	St. Ervan, Corn.
St. Eval	St. Eval, Corn. (A Breton saint whose name may derive from the Latin word for humble).
St. Ewe	St. Ewe, Corn.
St. Fechin	St. Vigeans, Angus.
St. Felix	Felixstowe, Suff.
St. Fergus	St. Fergus, St. Fergus Moss, A'deen.
St. Finian	St. Fillans, Perth: St. Finian's Bay, Kerry: Ardfinnan, Tipperary: Inisfallen, Kerry.
St. Florence	St. Florence, Pembs.
St. Gadoga	Llangadog, Carm. (A British saint of the 5th century who died in Brittany.)
St. George	St. George, Glam: St. George's, Corn: Ogbourne St. George, Wilts.
St. Genesius	St. Gennys, Corn.
St. German	St. Germain's Halt, I.O.M.: St. Germans, Corn.
St. Giles	St. Giles in the Heath, St. Giles in the Wood, Dev: St. Giles House, Dor: St. Giles Hill, Winchester: St. Giles, Oxford. Many important fairs were held in mediaeval times on his feast day—1st Sept.
St. Glywyatus	St. Gluvais, Corn.
St. Govan	St. Govans Head, Pemb.
St. Gowan	St. Gowan, Lightship.
St. Gwen	St. Wenn, Corn. from Cornish word meaning white.
St. Gwennarth	St. Weonards, Heref.
St. Gwynne	St. Gwynno Forest, Glam.
St. Harmon	St. Harmon, Radnor.
St. Helena	St. Helena, Norf.
St. Helen	St. Helen Aukland, Dur: St. Helens, Lancs/ Scilly/I.O.W.
St. Helerius	St. Helier, Jersey, C.I.
St. Hilary	St. Hilary, Corn/Glam.
St. Hippolytus	Ippollitts, Herts.
St. Idloes	Llanidloes, Mont.
St. Illtyd	St. Illtyd, Mon: Llanilltyd, Glam: Illston, Glam.
St. Ishmael	St. Ishmael, Pemb.
St. Issey	St. Issey, Mevagissey, Corn.
St. James	St. James, South Elmham, Suff.

St. John	St. Johns, Corn/Durham/Worcs: St. John's Beck, Cumb: St. John's chapel, Dur: St. John's Fen End, Norf: St. John's Head, Hoy, Orkney: St. John's Highway, Norf: St. John's Jerusalem, Kent: St. John's Lock, Caith/Glos: St. John's Point, Caith: St. John's Point, Donegal: St. John's Town of Dalry, Kirkcud.
St. Jude	St. Jude, I.O.M.
St. Just	St. Just in Penwith, St. Just in Roseland, Corn.
St. Kenelm	St. Kenelm's Well (A Mercian prince murdered at the age of seven by his aunt.)
St. Kevern	St. Keverne, Corn.
St. Kew	St. Kew, Corn.
St. Keyne	St. Keyne, Corn. Derived from a Welsh feminine name for beautiful.
St. Kilda	St. Kilda, Ross.
St. Lawrence	St. Lawrence, Corn/Essex/I.O.W.
St. Leonard	St. Leonards, Bucks/Dorset: St. Leonards Forest, Sussex.
St. Leger	Ashby St. Ledgers, Northants.
St. Levan	St. Levan, Corn.
St. Mabyn	St. Mabyn, Corn.
St. Magnus	St. Magnus Bay, Shetland.
St. Margaret	St. Margarets, Heref: St. Margaret's at Cliffe, Kent: St. Margaret's Bay, Kent: St. Margaret's Hope, Fife/Orkney: St. Margaret South Elmham, Suff.
St. Martin	St. Martin, Corn/Perth/Salop/Point Guernsey, C.I.
St. Mary	St. Mary Bourne, Hants: St. Mary Church, Glam: St. Mary Hill, Glam: St. Mary in the Marsh, Kent: St. Marylebone, London: St. Mary's Corn/Orkney/Sussex: St. Mary's Airfield, Scilly: St. Mary's Bay, Kent.
St. Maud	St. Mawes, Corn: St. Mawes Castle, Corn. St. Mawgan, Corn.
St. Mellion	St. Mellion, Mullion, Corn.
St. Mellous	St. Mellous, Mon.
St. Menefreda	St. Minver, Corn.
St. Merryn	St. Merryn, Corn.
St. Mevan	St. Mewan, Corn.
St. Michael	St. Michael Caerhays, Corn: St. Michaels, Kent/Worcs: St. Michael's Mount, Corn: St. Michael's on Wyre, Lancs.

St. Mochta	St. Mochta's House, C. Louth.
St. Moinenn	St. Monance, Fife.
St. Mullin	St. Mullins, Carlow.
St. Nechtan	St. Nighton, Corn.
St. Neot	St. Neot, Corn: St. Neots, Hunts.
St. Nicholas	St. Nicholas, Glam/Pemb: St. Nicholas at Wade, Kent.
St. Ninian	St. Ninians, Stir: St. Ninians Chapel, Wig: St. Ninians Isle, Shetland: St. Ninians Point, Bute.
St. Onens	St. Onens Bay, Jersey, C.I.
St. Osyth	St. Osyth, Essex: St. Osyth Marsh, Essex.
St. Owen	St. Owen's Cross, Heref.
St. Padern	Llanbadern, Rad/Card.
St. Patrick	St. Patrick's Isle, I.O.M.: Downpatrick, Down.
St. Peris	Llanberis, Caerns.
St. Peter	St. Peter Port, Guernsey, C.I.: St. Peters, Kent: St. Peter's Flat, Essex.
St. Petroc	St. Petrox, Pemb: Petrockstow, Devon: Padstow, Corn. (One of St. Patrick's missionary bishops.)
St. Piran	Perranzabuloe, Corn. (St. Perran in Sabulo = St. Perran in the drifting sand). An abbot consecrated by St. Patrick for a mission to Cornwall.
St. Pynocus	St. Pinnock, Corn.
St. Quivox	St. Quivox, Ayr.
St. Radigund	St. Radigund's Abbey, Kent.
St. Sampson	St. Sampson's, Guernsey, C.I.
St. Serf	St. Serf's Island, Kinross.
St. Stephen	St. Stephen's (3 places), Corn: St. Stephen's Coombe, Corn.
St. Tetha	St. Teath, Corn.
St. Tudno	Llandudno, Caerns.
St. Tudwal	St. Tudwald's Islands, Caern: St. Tudwald's Road, Caern.
St. Tudy	St. Tudy, Cornwall.
St. Twynnell	St. Twynnells, Pemb.
St. Vepus	St. Veep, Corn.
St. Weonard	St. Weonards, Heref.
St. Yvo	St. Ives, Corn/Hants/Hunts.: St. Ives Bay, Corn.

St. Acca	Hexham	St. Justus	Canterbury
St. Alban	St. Albans	St. Kenelm	Winchcombe
St. Aldhelm	Malmesbury	St. Lambert	Canterbury
St. Alkmund	Derby	St. Laurence	Canterbury
St. Amphibalus	St. Albans	St. Lewinna	Lewes
St. Augustine	Canterbury	St. Margaret	originally
St. Bede	Jarrow	(Queen of	Dunfermline
St. Birinus	Dorchester	Scotland)	
St. Boniface	Brixworth	St. Melangell	·Pennant
St. Brithwald	Canterbury		Melangell
St. Candida	Whitechurch	St. Mellitus	Canterbury
	Canonicorum	St. Mildred	Canterbury
St. Caradoc	St. Davids	St. Ninian	Withern,
St. Chad	Lichfield		Wigtown
St. Columba	Iona	St. Nothelm	Canterbury
St. Cuthbert	Durham	St. Odo	Canterbury
St. David	St. Davids	St. Osana	Howden
St. Deusdedit	Canterbury	St. Osmund	Salisbury
St. Dubricius	Llandaff	St. Oswald	Worcester
St. Dunstan	Canterbury/	St. Oswald	Durham
	Glastonbury	(King)	
St. Eanswythe	Folkestone	St. Oswin	Tynemouth
St. Edmund	Bury St.	St. Paulinus	Rochester
	Edmunds	St. Richard	Chichester
St. Edward	Westminster	John Schorne	North
(Confessor)			Marston
St. Egwin	Evesham	St. Swithin	Winchester
St. Erkenwald	St. Paul's	St. Tatwine	Canterbury
	London	St. Teilo	Llandaff/
St. Ethelbert	Hereford		Llandelio
St. Etheldreda	Ely		Fawr/Penaly,
St. Frideswide	Oxford		Tenby
St. Guthlac	Crowland	St. Theodore	Canterbury
St. Honorius	Canterbury	St. Thomas a	Canterbury
St. Hugh	Lincoln	Becket	
St. Hugh	Lincoln	St. Werberga	Chester/East
(Boy Martyr)			Dereham
St. John	Lincoln	St. Wilfred	Canterbury
Dalderby		St. William	Rochester
St. Judoc	Winchester	St. William	York
	(Hyde Abbey)	St. Wulfstan	Worcester
St. Justin	Llaniestyn,		
	Anglesey		

Air hostesses	St. Bona, V.
Archers	St. Sebastian, M.
Architects	St. Barbara, V.M.
Artillerymen	St. Barbara, V.M.
Bakers	St. Honorius. B.C.
Barbers	St. Cosmas, M.
Bee keepers	St. Bartholomew, Ap.
Bookbinders	St. John the Evangelist, Ap. Ev.
Brewers	St. Adrian, M. and St. Amand, B.C.
Bridge-builders	St. John of Nepomuck.
Carpenters and Joiners	St. Joseph, C.
Champions	St. Drausinus, B.C.
Children	St. Nicholas, B.C. and St. Ursula, V.M.
Cobblers	St. Euseus, C.
Cooks	St. Laurence, M.
Crossbowmen	St. Christopher, M.
Drapers	St. Ursula, V.M.
Dyers	St. Maurice, M.
Embroiderers	St. Clarus, M.
Farriers	St. John the Baptist.
Firework-makers	St. Barbara, V.M.
Fishmongers	St. Magnus, M.
Gardeners	St. Urban of Langres, B.C. and St. Fiacre, C.
Glaziers	St. James Allemanmus, C. and St. Mark, Ev.
Goldsmiths	St. Dunstan, B.C.
Grooms	St. Ann, W.
Hatters	St. Clement, P.M.
Hoodmakers	St. Severus, B.C.
Horse-soldiers	St. George, M.
Hunters	St. Hubert, B.C. and St. Eustachius, M.
Husbandmen	St. Walstan, C.
Innkeepers	St. Theodotus, M.
Lawyers	St. Yvo, C.
Locksmiths	St. Eligius, B.C.
Masons	St. Thomas, Ap. and St. Betesus, C.
Millers	St. Arnold, C. and St. Victor of Marseilles, C.
Miners (in Cornwall)	St. Kieran or Pieran, C.
Mowers	St. Walstan, C.

Musicians	St. Cecily, V.M.; St. Gregory Great, P.C.D.; St. Germanus of Paris, B.C.; St. Odo of Cluny, Ab.; St. Aldric, B.C.; St. Dunstan, B.C.
Navigators or Sailors	St. Nicholas, B.C.; St. Christopher, M.; St. Peter Gonzales of Elmo, C.
Notaries	St. Mark, Ev.
Painters	St. Luke, Ev. and St. Lazarus, C.
Papermakers	St. John the Evangelist, Ap. Ev.
Peasants	St. Lucy, V.M.
Philosophers	St. Catherine, V.M.
Physicians	Sts. Cosmas and Damian, MM. and St. Pantaleon, M.
Potters	St. Goar, C. and St. Fiacre, C.
Ropemakers	St. Paul, Ap. and St. Catherine, V.M.
Saddlers	St. Gualfard, H.
Servingmaids	St. Zita, V.
Shepherds	St. Wendelin, C. and St. Drugo, C.
Shoemakers	Sts. Crispin and Crispinian, MM.
Smiths	St. Eligius, B.C.
Soldiers	St. George, M.
Spinsters	St. Catherine, V.M.
Stonemasons	St. Reinoldus, C. and St. Blaise, B.M.
Students	St. Jerome, C.D.; St. Laurence, M.; St. Mathurin, C.; St. Mary Magdalen, Pent.; St. Catherine, V.M.; St. Gregory the Great, P.C.D.
Tailors	St. Homobonus, C.; St. John the Baptist; St. Lucy, V.M.
Tapestry Weavers	St. Francis, C.
Theologians	St. Thomas Aquinas, C.D.
Tilemakers	St. Fiacre, C.
Tin miners	St. Piran, Ab.
Travellers	St. Julian Hospitator, C. and St. Christopher.
Vine dressers	St. Urban, P.M. and St. Urban of Langres, B.C.
Washerwomen	St. Hunna.
Waxchandlers	St. Nicholas, B.C.
Weavers	Sts. Crispin and Crispinian, MM.; St. Stephen, M.; St. Arregondes.
Woolcombers	St. Blaise, M.

Aberdeen	St. Machan, B.C.
Buckingham	St. Rumbold, C.
Burton-upon-Trent	St. Modwena, V. Ab.
Cambray	St. John the Baptist and St. Maximilian.
Canterbury	St. Anselm, B.C.
Chester	St. Werberga, V. Abbess.
Colchester	St. Helen, Empress.
Cork (Diocese)	St. Finbar, B.C.
Crowland	St. Guthlac, H.
Derby	St. Alkmund, M.
Derry (Diocese)	St. Columb, B.C. and St. Eugene, B.C.
Dublin (Diocese)	St. Laurence, B.C.
Durham	St. Cuthbert, B.C.
Edinburgh	St. Giles, Ab.
England	B. Virgin Mary; St. Michael, Archl.; St. George, M.; St. Thomas of Canterbury, B.M.; St. Edward, K.C.
Folkestone	St. Eanswede, V. Ab.
Glasgow	St. Kentigern or Mungho, C.
Glastonbury	St. Joseph of Arimathea, C.
Hampstead	B. Virgin Mary.
Hereford	B. Virgin Mary.
Ireland	St. Patrick, B.C. and St. Bridget, V. Abbess.
Kildare (Diocese)	St. Conleth, B.C. and St. Bridget, Abbess.
Kilkenny	St. Canicus or Kenny, Ab.
Killaloe (Diocese)	St. Flanan, B.C.
Limerick (Diocese)	St. Muncain, B.C.
London	St. Paul, Ap.
Oxford	St. Frideswide, V.
Scotland	St. Andrew, Ap. and St. Margaret, Qu.
Tenterden	St. Mildreda, V. Ab.
Wales	St. David, B.C.

Anchor: St. Clement, P.M.; St. Felix, P.M.; St. Nicholas, B.C.
Anvil: in his hand—St. Adrian, M.
Apple: presenting to a king, and restoring him to sight—St. Malachy, B.C.
Archer: shooting her from the shore—St. Ursula, V.M.
Arm: his own burning in a fire—St. William Firmatus, H.
 his own cut off—St. Pelagius, M.
 holding up—St. Zegherus, O.PP.
Arrows: piercing him—St. Edmund, K.M.; St. Sebastian, M.
 piercing him on a gibbet—St. Anastasius, M.
 and knife—St. Otho, B.C.
 two arrows and sceptre—St. Edmund, K.M.
 two, offering them to heaven—St. Sebastian, M.
 two in hand, millstone by side—St. Christina, V.M.
 two, and a lance—St. Potentinus, M.
 three, in hand—St. Otho, B.C.
 bunch of, in hand—St. Sebastian, M.; St. Otho, B.C.; St. Faustus, M.
 quiver of, offering—St. Edmund, K.M.
 and bent bow—St. Mackessoge, B.C.
Axe: held in hand—St. Matthias, Ap.; St. Matthew, Ap. Ev.; St. Anastasius, M.; St. Proculus, M.; St. John Damascen, C.
 laid at the root of an oak—St. Boniface, B.M.
 held by Christ near him—St. Herman Joseph, C.
 fixed in his head—St. Josaphat, B.M.
 held in their hands—Sts. Martian and Malchus, two of the Seven Sleepers, MM.
 held in his hand—St. Rufus, B.M.
 and torch—St. Chrysanthus, M.
Ball: and chain near him—St. Jerom Emilian, C.
 of fire—St. Benedict, Ab.
Balls: three on a book, or in his hand—St. Nicholas, B.C.
 three in his lap, or at his feet—St. Nicholas, B.C.
 six, on a book—St. Nicholas, B.C.
 six, or nine, upon his shield—St. Quirinus, M.
Barge: St. Bertulphus, Ab.
Barrel: setting his archiepiscopal cross in it—St. Willebrord, B.C.
 shut up in—St. Antonia, V.M.
 near her—St. Antonia, V.M.
 eagle rising out of it—St. John, Ap. Ev.

MATTHEW

Evangelist

HUGH of AVALON...

BART EMEW

BONIFACE

ANTHONY

OSWALD

EDMUND

AIDAN

OSWIN

BLAISE

MATTHIAS

CATHERINE

EDWARD

CORFE

CUTHBERT

FAITH

ALBAN

MARK Ev.

CUTHBERT of LINDISFARNE

46

STEPHEN

JOHN Baptist...

John · Evangelist

JUDE

DAVID

G·I·L·E·S

JAMES

JAMES THE LESS.

GREAT

LAURENCE

PAUL

GT·ATHLAC

PETER

M

WERBERGA

O·S·MUND

NICHOLAS

B.V.M

WILLIAM

NORWICH

SIMON

EDWARD

CONFESSOR

DUNSTAN

VINCENT

PANCRAS

O·SYTH

LUKE

RICHARD·CHICHESTER

47

Basket, or baskets: in hand—St. John Damascen, C.
　　of bread in hand—St. Philip, Ap.
　　in hand—St. Joanna, Qu.
　　near her—St. Frances, W.
　　of eggs in hand—St. Rudbert, B.C.
　　of flowers or fruit in hand—St. Dorothy, V.M.
　　of fruit on arm—St. Sitha, V.
　　with a pitcher in it—St. Joanna.
　　with three apples and three roses, brought her by a
　　　　child—St. Dorothy, V.M.
　　of roses—St. Elizabeth of Hungary, Qu.W.
Bear: St. Humbert, C.
　　at his side—St. Maximinus, B.C.
　　keeping sheep—St. Florentius, B.C.
　　laden with baggage—St. Corcinian, B.C.
　　carrying wood for him—St. Gallus, C.
　　drawing a plough—St. James, B.C.
　　and crab tree—St. Mang, C.
　　and lion—St. Blandina, V.M.
　　seated before him—St. Edmund, K.M.
　　laying his hand on its head—St. Gallus, Ab. C.
　　licking his feet—St. Cerbonius, B.C.
　　fawning upon her—St. Columba, V.M.
　　held by a chain—St. Columba, V.M.
　　devouring a man at her feet—St. Columbina, V.
Beard: obtained by prayer—St. Wilgefortis, V.M.; St. Paula
　　Barbata, V.; St. Galla, V.
Beehive: St. Ambrose, B.C.D.; St. Bernard, C.D.; St. John
　　Chrysostom, B.C.D.
Bell: in hand—B. Mutius, Ab.
　　in hand or hung on staff—St. Anthony, Ab.
　　and fishes—St. Winwaloe, Ab.
　　two—St. Anthony, Ab.
Bellows: held by the devil—St. Genevieve, V.
Block: kneeling at—St. Fabian, P.M.
　　kneeling at, at sunrise—St. Waltheof, C.
Boat: in hand—St. Jude, Ap.
　　in her hand—St. Mary Magdalen, Penitent.
　　saint in it—St. Antoninus, B.C.; St. Are, B.C.
　　saint in it, with cloak for a sail—St. Raymond of Penna-
　　　　fort, C.
Boathook: St. Jude, Ap.
Boatman: in a barge—St. Julian Hospitator, Hermit.
Bodkin: in hand—St. Leodegarius or Leger, B.M.
　　long, in hand—St. Simon of Trent, M.
Bottle: and shears—St. Cosmas and Damian, MM.

Bound: to a tree—St. Sebastian, M.

Bowels: wound round a windlass—St. Erasmus, B.M.

Breasts: cut off, and lying in a dish—St. Agatha, V.M.
cut off, and variously tortured—St. Sophia and daughters, MM.

Bridge: standing upon or thrown from—St. John of Nepomucen, C.
and river near him—St. John Nepomucen, C.

Broom: in hand—St. Petronilla, V.

Bulls: dragged by—St. Thecla, V.M.

Burnt: to death—St. Polycarp, B.M.; St. Primatius, B.M.; St. Barnabas, Ap.; St. Timon, Deacon; Sts. Alexander and Apimachus, MM.; St. Thecla, V.M.; St. Eulalia, V.M.; St. Euphemia, V.M.; St. Zoa, M.; Sts. Potamiaena and Marcella, MM.

Candle: in her hand—St. Beatrix, V.M.

Cart: with wood—St. Marina, V.

Cauldron: boiled in—St. Afra, M.; St. Cecily, V.M.

Cave: cobweb over its entrance—St. Felix of Nola, C.

Chafing dish: St. Agatha, V.M.

Chain: broken in his hand—St. John of Matha, C.; St. Ferreolus, B.M.; St. Felix of Valois, C.
in his hand—St. Leonard, C.

Charcoal burner: or collier chosen bishop—St. Alexander Carbonarius, B.M.

Child: carrying Christ child on shoulder—St. Christopher, M.

Church: in his hand—St. Jerome, C.D.; St. Nicholas, B.C.; St. Ludger, B.C.; St. Lawrence, M.; St. Geminianus, B.C.; St. Cunibert, B.C.; St. Delphinus, B.C.; St. Robert of Newminster, Ab. C..; St. Sebaldus, Hermit; St. Virgilius, B.C.; St. Leopold IV of Austria; St. Amandus, B.C.; St. Godfrey, C.; St. Wolfgang, B.C.; St. Severinus, B.C.; St. Vitalian, B.C.; St. Fulgentius, B.C.; St. William of Eskille, Ab. C.; St. Botolph, Ab.

Cloak: divided with a poor man—St. Martin, B.C.
spread out before him—St. Alban, M.
sailing upon it on the sea—St. Hyacinth, C.
standing upon it on the sea—St. Francis of Paula, C.
crossing the Danube upon—St. Sebaldus, K.H.
hung on a sunbeam—St. Gothard, B.C.

Club: in hand—St. Eugenius, M.; St. Telesphorus, P.M.; Sts. John Constantine and Maximian, MM. (of the Seven Sleepers); St. Fabian, P.M.; St. Boniface, B.M.; St. Andreolus, M.

Coals: St. Tiburtius, M.
  hot in his lap, vestment or hand—St. Brice, B.C.
  walking over—St. Salvator ab Horta, C.
  standing or sitting upon—St. Apollinaris, B.M.
Combs: torn with—St. Blaise, B.M.
Corn: ear of—St. Fara, V.
  three or five ears of—St. Walburge, Abbess.
Cow: wild by her side—St. Perpetua, M.
  red by her side—St. Modwena, V. Abbess.
Crocodile: under his feet—St. Theodore, B.C.
Cross: tall T., or triple in hand—St. Philip, Ap.; St. Matthew,
    Ap.; St. Michael, Archangel; St. Nestor, B.M.; St. Alban,
    M.; St. Francis of Assisi; St. Didacus, C.
  in hand—St. Hedwiges, W.; St. Agnes, V.M.; St. Eulalia,
    V.M.; St. Thecla, V.M.
  with cap and wallet; St. Bridget, W.
  inverted, carrying; St. Jude, Ap.
Dagger: St. Olaus or Olave, K.M.
  and sceptre, cup or falcon—St. Edward, K.M.
  and sword—St. Kilian, B.M.
  and palm—St. Bibiana, V.M.; St. Agnes, V.M.
Dish: silver, broken up to relieve the poor—St. Oswald, K.M.
Distaff: in her arms—St. Rosalia, V.
  spinning with—St. Genevieve, V.
Dog: at feet—St. Bernard, Ab. D.;St. Wendelin, C.
  near him—St. Benignus, M.
  with a loaf in his mouth or licking wounds—St. Rock, C.
Doorway: standing in—St. Anthony, Ab. C.
Dragged: by a horse—St. Tryphon, M.
  by wild horses—Sts. Martinian and Saturian, MM.
  by the neck—St. Mark, Ev.
  by her feet and stoned—St. Cointha, V.M.
Dragon: by side, or pierced with his spear, or sword—St.
    George, M.; St. Michael, Archangel.
  by her side—St. Margaret, V.
  killed with a cross—St. Florentinus Vindemialis, B.C.
  held by him in a chain—St. Sylvester, Pope. C.; St. John
    of Rheims, C.
Eagle: before or above him; St. John, Ap. Ev.
  before him—Gregory the Great, P.C.D.
  sheltering him from rain—St. Bertulph, Ab.; St. Medard,
    B.C.
  fanning him sleeping in the sun—St. Servatius, B.C.
  bearing him on its back—St. John, Ap. Ev.
Eel: given to a poor man, turning into gold: St. Spiridion, B.C.

Eyes: in a dish or on a book—St. Lucy, V.M.
on a book, or at her feet—St. Othilia, V.
his own, before him—St. Goeric, B.C.
plucked out, and hands cut off—St. Mennas, M.
plucked out—St. Leodegarius or Leger, B.M.
carrying them—St. Trophymus, M.
of executioner dropping out—St. Alban, M.
Feet: nailed to the ground—St. Tryphon, M.
Ferrying: travellers over a river—St. Julian Hospitator, C.
Fish: in his hand—St. Raphael, Archl; B. Nicholas, O.P.
or two fishes—St. Simon, Ap.
Fish-hooks: holding—St. Zeno, M.
Flail: St. Varus, M.
Flames: hung over, with head downwards—St. Agapetus, M.
burning in—St. Primatius, B.M.
praying in—St. Januarius, B.M.
walking on—St. Anthony, Ab.
stabbed in—St. Polycarp, B.M.
on his left—Uriel, Archangel.
Flies: stinging him in the desert—St. Macarius, C.
Foot: cut off—St. Victor of Marseilles, M.; St. Victorinus, M.
Footmarks: imprinting in a stone—St. Medard, B.C.
Frogs: about him—St. Huvar or Hervaeus, Ab.; St. Rieul, C.
Gardener: with a spade—St. Phocas, M.; St. Salvator, Ab.;
St. Horta, C.
Gibbett: hanged upon—St. Colman, M.
pierced with arrows upon—St. Anastasius, M.
near him—St. Ferreolus, B.M.
Glove: and staff—St. Bavo, Anchorite.
Gourd bottle: Raphael, Archl.
Grid-iron: St. Laurence, M.; St. Cyprian, M.; St. Eustratius,
M.; St. Donatilla, M.; Sts. Macedonius and Theodulus,
MM.
bowels on—St. Erasmus, B.M.
set with spikes—St. Vincent, M.
or iron bed and sword—St. Faith, V.M.
Hail: striking down her torturers—St. Catherine, V.M.
Halberd: St. Matthias, Ap.; St. Matthew, Ap.; St. Jude, Ap.
and loaf—St. Holofius or Olave, K.M.
Hammer: in his hand—St. Reinoldus   C.; St. Adrian, M.
and sword—St. Adrian, M.
in one hand, three nails in the other—St. William of
Norwich, M.
and chalice—St. Eligius, B.C.
Hand: cut off, held in the other—St. Quiriacus, B.M.; St.
John Damascen, B.C.

Harp: St. Dunstan, B.C.; St. Cecily, V.M.
Hatchet: St. Matthias, Ap.; St. Matthew, Ap.; St. Wolfgang, B.C.; St. Adjutus, B.C.
Heart: in his hand—St. Francis of Sales, B.C.; St. Augustine, B.C.D.; St. Rumold, B.M.
Hoe: a man with, behind him/or rake in his hand—St. Isidore of Madrid, C.
Hook: St. Eulalia, V.M.; St. Filician, B.M.; St. Vincent, M.; St. Agatha, V.M.
    with double prongs—St. Leodegarius, B.M.
Horse: standing by him—St. Severus of Abranches, B.C.; St. Barochus, C.
    dragged by—St. Tryphon, M.; St. Ivan, Hermit; St. Hippolytus, M.; St. Quirinus, M.
Hour-glass: holding—St. Hilarion, Ab.
Iron: hot, applied to her breast—St. Calliopa, V.M.
Jug, or ewer: in his hand—St. Vincent, M.
Key: or two keys in his hand—St. Peter, Ap.
    in his hand—St. Servatius, B.C.; St. Benignus, M.
    and clasped book—St. Petronilla, V.
King: with a cross on his breast—St. Ferdinand, K.C.
Lamb: at her feet—St. Agnes, V.M.; St. Regina, V.M.
Lamb's foot: St. John the Baptist.
Lamp: St. Macarius of Alexandria, C.
Lance: or spear—St. Gengulph, M.; St. Hippolytus, M.; Canute K.M.
Lantern: St. Hugh, B.C.
    devil trying to extinguish—St. Gudula, V.
Lead: molten poured over him—St. Erasmus, B.M.
    poured into his mouth—St. Primus, M.
Lion: by his side—St. Adrian, M.; St. Jerome, C.D.; St. Mark, Ev.
Lock: on his lips—St. Raymund Nonnatus, C.
Locksmith's tools: St. Galmier, C.; St. Apelles, H.
Mill: or mortar, bruised in—St. Victorinus, M.
Millstone: about her neck, thrown in to the sea—St. Auren, V
    about her neck, or by her—St. Christina, V.M.
    tied to his neck—St. Callixtus, P.M.; St. Quirinus, B.M.
    and sword—St. Victor of Marseilles, M.
Nail: in his head—St. Julian of Emesa, M.
    in his head and hand—St. Severus of Rome, M.
    through his hands into his head—St. Panteleon, M.
Nails: forging out of arrows—St. Otho, B.C.
Oak: felled by a bishop—St. Boniface, B.M.
Oar: St. Jude, Ap.; St. Julian Hospitator, H.
Organ: St. Cecily, V.M.

Ox: St. Luke, Ev. .

Padlock: on his lips—St. John Nepomucen, C.

Painting box and brush: St. Herman Joseph, C.

Palm: and cup—St. John, Ap. Ev.

and banner—St. Julian, B.M.

Pen: hand passing it to him—St. Basil, B.C.D.

Penknife: St. Herman Joseph, C.

Penknives: martyred with—St. Cassian, M.

Pick axe: in his hand—St. Leodegarius or Leger, B.M.

Pig: by his side—St. Anthony, Ab.

Pig's head: St. Blaise, B.M.

Pilgrim: with staff, hat, shell, wallet, some, or all of them—

St. James the Greater, Ap.

with staff—Raphael, Archl.

with staff and book—St. Fridolin, Ab.

with crucifix staff—St. Jodoc, H.

crown at his feet—St. Richard, K.C.

Pincers: or locksmith's tools—St. Galmier, C.

red hot—St. Pelagius, M.

torn by—St. Agatha, V.M.

held in her hand—St. Lucy, V.M.; St. Apollonia, V.M.

tooth held in them—St. Apollonia, V.M.

Plough: held by him—St. Exuperius, B.C.; St. Richard, B.C.

drawn by stags—St. Ecian or Echenus, B.C.; St. Robert

(of Dale Abbey)

Ploughshares: red hot, walking over—St. Cunegundes, Empress

Post: tied to it—St. Agricola, M.

Prison bars: saint seen through—St. Martin, P.M.

Purses: three—St. Nicholas, B.C.

Rack: stretched upon—St. Vincent, M.; St. Areadius, M.

Rake: or hoe in hand—St. Isidore of Madrid, C.

Razor: in hand—St. Pamphilius, M.

on a book—St. Landry, B.C.

Reaping corn: for bread for the altar—St. Wenceslas, M.

Rings: iron on his neck and arms—St. Theodosius, C.

seven on right hand—St. Gertrude, V. Abbess.

Saddle: near him—St. Eligius, B.C.

Salmon: with a ring in its gills—St. Kentigern, B.C.

Saw: St. Simon, Ap.; St. James, the Less, Ap.

Sawed off: her hands and feet—St. Fausta, V.M.

Scales: weighing souls in them—St. Michael, Archl.

Schoolmaster: St. Maws, B.C.

Scourge: St. Ambrose, B.C.D.; St. Boniface, B.M.

Scythe: St. Walstan, C.; St. Valentius, M.

and a well—St. Sidwell, V.M.

Serpent: rising out of a cup or chalice—St. John, Ap. Ev.

Serpents: treading upon—St. Didymus, M.; St. Patrick, B.C.
Shell: escallop in his hand, or on his hat, cloak, or wallet—St. James the Greater, Ap.
Shepherd: with a dog at his feet—St. Wendelin, Ab.
Ship: with sails in his hand—St. Jude, Ap.
Shoes: in her hand—St. Hedwige W.
    with spikes through them—St. Sozon, M.
Shoemakers: two at work—Sts. Crispin and Crispinian, MM.
Shovel: baker's—St. Honorius, B.C.
Sickle: St. Nothburge, V.
Sieve: St. Hippolytus, M.
Spade: St. Fiacre, C.
Sparrow: St. Dominic, C.
Spider: over a chalice—St. Conrad, B.C.
Square: carpenter's or builder's—St. Joseph, C.; St. Jude, Ap.; St. Matthew, Ap.; St. Thomas, Ap.; St. Mathias, Ap.
Stocks: prisoners released from—St. Leonard, C.
Stones: St. Stephen, M.
Sun: on his breast—St. Thomas Aquinas, C.D.
    and stars on his breast—St. Nicholas of Tolentinum, C.
Sunbeam: his cloak hung upon: standing before a bishop—St. Gothard, B.C.
Swan: St. Hugh of Grenoble, B.C.
Sword: St. Paul, Ap.; St. James the Greater, Ap.; St. Secundus, H.; St. Dominic, C.
Teeth: pulled out—St. Apollonia, V.M.
Thistle: holding—St. Narcissus, B.C.
Unicorn: at feet—St. Justina, V.M.
Vane: St. Leonard, C.
Violin: St. Genesius, M.
    angel playing to him—St. Francis of Assisi, C.
Wagon: carrying—St. Bavo, C.
    standing in—St. Francis of Assisi, C.
Weight: fastened to her feet—St. Flavia, M.
    lying by her feet—St. Nothburge, V.
Well: thrown into—St. Gereon, M.; St. Callixtus, P.M.; St. Sebastian, M.
Wheel: St. Catherine, V.M.; St. Euphemia, V.M.
    tied on, breasts cut off, liver torn out—St. Encratida, V.M.
    white, on a red ground—St. Willigis, B.C.
    and sword, or wheels broken—St. Catherine, V.M.
    set round with lights—St. Donatus, B.M.
    broken at his feet—St. Quintin, M.
Woolcards: or woolcomb—St. Blaise, B.M.

A CALENDAR OF SAINTS

The saints recorded in this list have been collected from various ecclesiastical calendars—e.g. Sarum, Old English, Scottish, French, Spanish, Greek, German and Roman. Among the different usages we can find many alternative dates and those recorded below are the ones usually observed in Britain.

JANUARY
1st   Sts. Elvan, B. and Mydwyn, in England, c. 198.
2nd Holy Martyrs of Lichfield, c. 304.
3rd   St. Melor, Cornwall, c. 411
4th   St. Rumon, Tavistock, before 960. A bishop.
5th   St. Edward the Confessor, King of England, 1066.
6th   St. Peter, Abp. of Canterbury, 606.
7th   St. Cedd, B. of London, 664.
8th   St. Pega, V., c. 718, sister of St. Guthlac of Crowland.
9th   Sts. Adrian, 709, and Britwald, 731. Abps. of Canterbury.
10th St. Nicanor, 76, one of the first seven deacons.
11th St. Egwin, B. of Worcester, 720.
12th St. Benedict Biscop, 703.
13th St. Kentigern, B. of Glasgow, 601.
14th St. Datius, B. of Milan, 552.
15th St. Ytha, V. in Ireland, 6th cent.
16th St. Henry, H. in Northumberland, 1127.
17th St. Mildgitha, V. in Kent, c. 750.
18th St. Face, C. at Cremona, 1272.
19th St. Wulstan, B. of Worcester, 1095.
20th St. Fechin, Ab. at Fore in Ireland, 665.
21st St. Agnes, V.M. at Rome, 303.
22nd St. Brithwald, B. of Wilton, 1045.
23rd St. Boisilus, of Melrose, c. 664.
24th St. Cadoc, Ab. & M., M. Wales, 6th cent.
25th St. Poppo, Ab. of Stavelot in Belgium, 1048.
26th St. Theoritgitha, V. at Barking, Essex, 7th cent.
27th St. Vitalian, Pope, 671.
28th St. Cyril, Patriarch of Alexandria, 445.
29th St. Gildas the Wise, Ab. in Brittany, 6th cent.
30th St. Hyacintha, V. at Viterbo, 1640.
31st St. Serapion, M. among the Moors, 1240. An Englishman.

FEBRUARY
1st   St. Bridget, V. & Abs. at Kildare, 525.
2nd St. Laurence, Abp. of Canterbury, 619.

3rd St. Blaise, B. M. at Sebaste, c. 316.
4th St. Gilbert of Sempringham, Ab., 1189.
5th St. Agatha, V.M. at Catania, 251.
6th St. Ina, King of West Saxons, c. 730.
7th St. Augulus, B.M. in London.
8th St. Cuthman, C. at Steyning, Sussex. Native of Devon/
Cornwall.
9th St. Teilo, B. of Llandaff, c. 560.
10th St. Scholastica, V. at Monte Cassino, 543.
11th St. Ceadmon, Monk at Whitby, c. 680.
12th St. Ethelwold, B. of Lindisfarne, 740.
13th St. Catherine of Ricci. V. 1589.
14th St. Valentine, M. at Rome, 269.
15th St. Berach, B. in Ireland, 615.
16th St. Onesimus, Disciple of St. Paul, 95.
17th St. Finian, B. of Lindisfarne, 661.
18th St. Simeon, B.M. of Jerusalem, 107.
19th St. Odran, M. in Ireland, 451.
20th St. Mildred, V. Abs. in Thanet, c. 700.
21st St. Gondebert, B. of Sens, France, 7th cent.
22nd St. Margaret of Cortona, 1297.
23rd St. Milburga, V. Abs. of Wenlock, Salop, 7th cent.
24th St. Ethelbert, King of Kent, 616.
25th St. Walburgis, V. Abs. of Heidenheim, 780.
26th St. Porphry, B. of Gaza, 421.
27th St. Alnoth, H.M. in England, c. 727.
28th St. Proterius, M. Patriarch of Alexandria, 457.
29th St. Oswald, Abp. of York, 992. The only saint commemorated on this day.

MARCH
1st St. David, Abp. Patron Saint of Wales, 544.
2nd St. Chad, B. of Lichfield, 672.
3rd St. Winwaloe, Ab. of Landvenec, Brittany, 6th cent.
4th St. Owen, Monk of Lastingham, 7th cent.
5th St. Piran (Perran) Ab. in Cornwall, 6th cent.
6th St. Fridolin, Ab. of Sickingen, 7th cent.
7th St. Easterwin, Ab. of Wearmouth, 785.
8th St. Felix, B. of East Saxons, 654.
9th St. Bosa, B. in Northumbria, 705.
10th St. Kessog, B. in Scotland, 4th cent.
11th St. Constantine, King, Monk & M., Scotland, 576.
12th St. Alphege the Bald, B. of Winchester, 951.
13th St. Kennocha, V. in Scotland, c. 1007.
14th St. Lubin, B. of Chartres, 557.
15th St. Magorian, C. at Trent, 5th cent.

16th   St. Finian the Leper, Ab. of Inisfathlen, Ireland, c. 610.
17th   St. Joseph of Arimathea, 1st cent.
       St. Patrick, B. Apostle of Ireland, 460.
18th   St. Edward, K.M., 978.
19th   St. Alkmund, M. at Derby, 800.
20th   St. Cuthbert, B. of Lindisfarne, 685.
21st   St. Benedict, Ab. of Monte Cassino, 543.
22nd   Blessed Thomas of Lancaster, M. at Pontefract, 1321.
23rd   Sts. Fingar and Piala, W. MM. in Cornwall, c. 484.
24th   St. Hildelitha, V. Abs. of Barking, Essex, c. 720.
25th   The Penitent Thief, 33.
       St. William, Child M. at Norwich, 1144.
26th   St. Mochelloc, Ab. in Ireland, c. 650.
27th   St. Matthew of Beauvais, M. in France, 11th cent.
28th   St. Guntram, K. of Burgundy, 593.
29th   St. Gundleus (Gwynllyn Filwr), K.H. in Wales, c. 529.
30th   St. John in the Well, H. in Armenia.
31st   St. Daniel, C. at Venice, 1411.

APRIL

1st   St. Gilbert, B. of Caithness, c. 1211.
2nd   St. Musa, V. at Rome, 6th cent.
3rd   St. Richard, B. of Chichester, 1253.
       St. Pancras, B.M. of Taormina, Sicily, 1st cent.
4th   St. Gwerir, H. at Ham Stoke, Cornwall, 9th cent.
5th   St. Vincent Ferrier, C. O.S.D. at Vannes, Brittany, 1419.
6th   St. Bertham, B. of Kirkwall, Orkney, c. 839.
7th   St. Aphraates, H. in Syria, 4th cent.
8th   St. Dionysius, B. of Corinth, c. 180.
9th   St. Waltrudis, Abs. at Mons, Belgium, 7th cent.
10th   St. Fulbert, B. of Chartres, 1028.
11th   St. Guthlac, M. at Crowland, Lincs, 714.
12th   St. Zeno, B. of Verona, 4th cent.
13th   St. Winock, B. in Scotland, c. 875.
       St. Justin the Apologist, M. at Rome, 167.
14th   St. Benet of the Bridge, C. at Avignon, 1184.
15th   St. Ruadan, Ab. of Lothra, Ireland, 6th cent.
16th   St. Magnus, Count of Orkney, M. 1110.
17th   St. Domnan, M. in Ewe Isle, Scotland, c. 600.
18th   St. Laserian, B. Ab. of Leighlin, Ireland, 639.
19th   St. Alphege, M. Abp. of Canterbury, 1012.
20th   St. Agnes, V., O.S.D. Monte Pulciano, 1317.
21st   St. Anselm, Abp. of Canterbury, 1109.
       St. Beuno, Ab. of Clynnog, Caerns., 7th cent.
22nd   St. Leo, B. of Sens, France, 540.

23rd St. George, M. at Lydda, Israel, 303, Patron Saint of England.
24th St. Mellitus, B. of London & Abp. of Canterbury, 624.
25th St. Mark the Evangelist, B. of Alexandria, c. 68.
St. Maughold, B. of Man., 5th cent.
26th St. Richarius, Ab. of Centule, France, 7th cent.
27th St. Zita, V. at Lucca, Italy, 1272.
28th St. Cronan, Ab. of Roscrea, Ireland, 615.
29th St. Hugh, Ab of Cluny, 1109.
30th St. Erkonwald, B. of London, 693.

MAY

1st St. Kellac, B. in Ireland, 7th cent.
St. Asaph, B. of Wales, 7th cent.
2nd St. Waldebert, Ab. of Luxeuil, 665.
3rd St. Aufried, B. of Utrecht, 1008.
4th St. Pelagia, M. at Tarsus, 3rd cent.
5th St. Hilary, B. of Arles, 449.
6th St. Eadbert, B. of Lindisfarne, 698.
7th St. John of Beverley, Abp. of York, 721.
8th St. Desideratus, B. of Bourges, 550.
9th St. Hermas, B. of Philippi, 1st cent.
10th St. Isidore the Husbandman, C. at Madrid, 1130.
11th St. Fremund, K.M. at Harbury, Warw., c. 795.
12th St. Pancras, M. at Rome, 304.
13th St. Loeldad, Ab. of Monaghan, 7th cent.
14th St. Halvard, M. in Norway, 11th cent.
15th St. Britwin, Ab. of Beverley, Yorks, 733.
16th St. Brendan, Ab. of Clonfert, 577.
St. Simon Stock, priest in England, 1265.
17th St. Madern, H. in Cornwall.
18th St. Conwal, Archdeacon of Glasgow, 7th cent.
19th St. Dunstan, Abp. of Canterbury, 988.
20th St. Ethelbert, K. of East Anglia, 793.
21st St. Godrick, H. at Finchale, Dur., 1170.
22nd St. Julia, V.M. in Corsica, 6th/7th cent.
23rd St. William of Rochester, M. in England.
24th Blessed John de Prado, M. in Morocco, 1336.
25th St. Aldhelm, B. of Sherborne, Dorset, 709.
26th St. Augustine, B. of Canterbury, Apostle of the English, 605.
27th St. Bede the Venerable, monk of Jarrow, 734.
28th Blessed Lanfranc, Abp. of Canterbury, 1089.
29th St. Burian, V. in Cornwall.

30th   St. Anastasius, B. of Pavia, 680.
31st   St. Lupicinus, B. of Verona, 6th cent.

JUNE

1st   St. Wistan, K.M. at Evesham, Worcs., 849.
2nd   St. Nicholas the Pilgrim, C. at Trani, 1096.
3rd   St. Kevin, Ab. at Glendalough, Ireland, 618.
4th   St. Petrock, Ab. at Bodmin, Corn., 600.
5th   St. Boniface, M. Abp. of Mainz, 755.
6th   St. Gudwall, B. in Cornwall, 7th cent.
7th   St. Robert, Ab. of Newminster, Yorks, 1159.
8th   St. William, Abp. of York, 1154.
9th   St. Columba, Ab. of Iona, 597.
10th   St. Ithamar, B. of Rochester, 656.
11th   St. Achas, boy at Thourhout, Belgium, 1220.
12th   St. Ternan, B. of Picts, Scotland, 431.
13th   St. Antony of Padua, O.M. in Italy, 1231.
14th   St. Aldate, B. of Gloucester, c. 500.
15th   St. Eadburga, V. at Winchester, Hants. c. 680.
16th   St. Aurelian, B. of Arles, 551.
17th   St. Botolph, Ab. of Boston, 655.
18th   Sts. Marcus and Marcellinus, MM. at Rome, c. 287.
19th   St. Odo, B. of Cambrai, 1113.
20th   St. Novatus, P. at Rome, 151.
21st   St. Meven, Ab. in Brittany, 6th cent.
22nd   St. Alban, M. at Verulam, Herts., c. 301
23rd   St. Etheldreda, C.V. Abs. of Ely, 629.
24th   St. Bartholomew, H. in the island of Farne, 1182.
25th   St. Molach, B. in Ross, Ireland, 7th cent.
26th   St. Dionysias, Abp. of Bulgaria, 1180.
27th   St. Crescens, disciple of St. Paul, c. 100.
28th   St. Pappian, M. at Mylas, Sicily.
29th   Sts. Peter and Paul, Apostles, MM. in Rome, 65.
30th   Blessed Raymond Lulli, M. in Africa, 1315.

JULY

1st   Sts. Julius and Aavon, MM. at St. Albans (Verulam), 304.
2nd   St. Ouduck, B.C.
3rd   St. Germain, B. in I.O.Man, 5th cent.
4th   St. Odo, Abp. of Canterbury, 958.
5th   St. Mongunna, V. Abs. in Ireland, c. 650.
6th   St. Morwenna, V. in Cornwall, 5th cent.
7th   St. Hedda, B. of East Saxons, 705.
8th   St. Edgar, K. of the English, 975.
9th   Sts. John Fisher and Thomas More.

10th   St. Canute, K.M. at Fyen, Denmark, 1086.
11th   St. Drostan, C. in Scotland, c. 600.
12th   St. Veronica, at Caesarea Philippi, 1st cent.
13th   St. Mildred, V. Abs. of Minster, Thanet, 8th cent.
14th   St. Bonaventura, B. of Alba, 1274.
15th   St. Swithin, B. of Winchester, 862, Translation.
       St. Donald and his nine daughters, VV. in Scotland, 716.
16th   St. Helier, M. in Jersey 6th cent.
17th   St. Kenelm, Boy M. at Winchcombe, Glos. 819.
18th   St. Thenew, M. in Scotland, 574.
19th   St. Vincent de Paul, C. at Paris, 1660.
20th   St. Wilgeforte (Uncumber), V. M. Portugal.
21st   St. Arbogast, B. of Strasburg, 678.
22nd   St. Mary Magdalene, Penitent in Palestine, 1st cent.
23rd   St. Apollinarius, B.M. at Ravenna, c. 75.
24th   Sts. Wulfhead and Rufin, MM. at Stone, Staffs., c. 658.
25th   St. Christopher, M. in Lycia, 3rd cent.
26th   St. Anne, Mother of the Blessed Virgin Mary.
27th   St. Hugh of Lincoln, M. 1255.
28th   St. Irene, V.Ab. at Constantinople, 10th cent.
29th   St. Olaf, K.M. in Norway, 1030.
30th   St. Tatwin, Abp. of Canterbury, 734.
31st   St. Neot, C. in Cornwall, c. 877.

AUGUST

1st   St. Justin, Boy M. at Paris.
      St. Almedha, V.M. at Brecknock, 6th cent.
      St. Ethelwold, B. of Winchester, 974.
2nd   St. Etheldritha, V. at Crowland, 623.
3rd   St. Waltheof, Ab. in Scotland, 1160.
4th   St. Molua, Ab. of Clonfert, Ireland, 606.
5th   St. Oswald, K.M. in Northumbria, 642.
6th   St. Acca, B. of Hexham, c. 740.
7th   St. Claudia, matron at Sabinum in Umbria, c. 110.
8th   St. Hormisdas, M. in Persia, 4th cent.
9th   St. Fedlimid, B. at Kilmore, Ireland, c. 550.
10th St. Laurence, M. at Rome, 258.
      St. Malchus, B. of Lismore, Ireland, 1130.
11th St. Susanna, V.M. at Rome, c. 295.
12th St. Muredach, B. of Killala, Ireland, 580.
      St. Clare, V. at Assisi, Umbria, 1253.
13th Blessed John Berchmans, S.J. at Rome, 1621.
14th St. Fachnan, B. of Rosscarbery, Ireland, 590.
15th St. Alypius, B. of Tagaste, Africa, c. 430.

16th   St. Roch, C. at Montpellier, France, 14th cent.
17th   St. James, Deacon at York, c. 650.
18th   St. Inan, C. at Irvine, Scotland, 9th cent.
       St. Helena, Empress at Constantinople, c. 328.
19th   St. Mochteus, B. of Louth, Ireland, 535.
20th   St. Oswin, K.M. of Northumbria, 651.
       St. Ronald, M. in Orkney, 1158.
21st   St. Leontius, B. of Bordeaux, 6th cent.
22nd St. Sigfrid, Ab. of Wearmouth, 689.
       St. Hippolytus, B.M. at Porto, Rome, 3rd cent.
23rd St. Justinian, H.M. at Ramsey, Pembs., c. 540.
24th   St. Bartholomew, Ap. M. in India, 50.
       St. Yarcard, B. in Scotland, c. 450.
25th   St. Ebba, V. Abs. at Coldingham, 683.
       St. Hilda, V. Abs. of Whitby, Yorks., 680.
26th   St. Breqwin, B.C. at Canterbury, 762.
27th   St. Decuman, H.M. near Dunster, Som., 706.
28th   St. Augustine, B. of Hippo, Africa, 430.
29th   St. Sebbi, K. of East Saxons, 694.
30th   St. Modan, H. at Kill-Modan, Ulster.
       St. Fiacre, H. at Breuil, France, 7th cent.
31st   St. Aidan, B. of Lindisfarne, 651.

SEPTEMBER

1st   St. Lupas, B. of Sens, 623.
2nd St. Justas, B. of Lyons, 390.
3rd St. Serapia, V.M. at Rome, 121.
4th   St. Monessa, V. in Ireland, c. 456.
5th   St. Bertinus, Ab. at St. Omer, c. 709.
6th   St. Bega or Bee, Abs. in Cumberland, 7th cent.
7th   St. Modoc, B. of Ferns, Scotland, 632.
8th   St. Ugo, B. of Volterra, Tuscany, 1184.
9th   St. Omer, B. in Artois, c. 670.
      St. Bertelin, H. at Stafford, 8th cent.
      St. Kieran, Ab. of Clonmacnois, Ireland, 548.
10th St. John of Salerno, C. at Florence, 13th cent.
11th Sts. Protus and Hyacinth, MM. at Rome, 262.
12th St. Guido, C. at Anderlecht, Brabant, 1012.
13th St. Philip, M. at Alexandria, 3rd cent.
14th St. John Chrysostom, B. of Constantinople, 407.
15th St. Catherine Flisca, W. at Genoa, 1510.
16th St. Edith, Abs. at Polesworth, c. 964.
      St. Edith, V. at Wilton, Wilts., 984.
17th Sts. Socrates and Stephen, MM. at Monmouth, c. 304.
18th St. Ferreolus, M. at Vienne, Gaul, c. 304.
19th St. Theodore, Abp. of Canterbury, 690.

20th	Sts. Eustathius, Theopista, Agapins and Theopistus, MM. at Rome, 118.
21st	St. Alexander, B.M. on the Claudian Way, Italy, 2nd cent.
	St. Matthew, Apostle M. in Ethiopia, 1st cent.
22nd	Sts. Diga and Emerita, MM. at Rome, 3rd cent.
23rd	St. Adamnan, Ab. of Iona, 704.
24th	St. Robert, H. at Knaresborough, Yorks., 1218.
25th	St. Finbar, B. of Cork, 623.
	St. Ceolfrid, Ab. of Wearmouth, 716.
26th	Sts. Cyprian and Justina, MM. at Nicomeda, 304.
27th	St. Zenas, disciple of St. Paul, 1st cent.
28th	St. Privatus, M. at Rome, 222.
	St. Wenceslas, K.M. in Bohemia, 936.
29th	St. Michael and All Angels.
30th	St. Honorus, Abp. of Canterbury, 653.

OCTOBER

1st	St. Michael and his Companions, Monks at Sebastápol, c. 788.
2nd	St. Leodegar or Leger, B.M. at Autun, 678.
	St. Thomas Cantilupe, B. of Hereford, 1282.
3rd	St. Romana, V.M. at Beauvais, c. 303.
4th	St. Francis of Assisi, c. 1226.
5th	St. Murdach, H. in Argyll.
6th	St. Yuri, D. at Wilton, Wilts., 7th cent.
7th	St. Osyth, V.M. at Chick, Essex, 7th cent.
8th	St. Keyne, V. in Abergavenny, Mon., c. 490.
9th	St. Robert Grostete, B. of Lincoln, 1253.
10th	St. John of Bridlington, C. in York, 1379.
11th	St. Kenny, Ab. of Kilkenny, Ireland, 599.
12th	St. Edwin, K. of Northumbria, 633.
	St. Wilfred, B. of York, 709.
13th	St. Edward the Confessor, K. at Westminster, 1066.
14th	St. Callixtus, Pope M. at Rome, 222.
15th	St. Leonard, C. at Autun, c. 576.
16th	St. Colman, B. of Killruadh, Ireland.
17th	St. Levan, B. in Cornwall, 6th cent.
	St. Nothelm, Abp. of Canterbury, 738.
	Sts. Ethelred and Ethelbert, MM. in Kent, 690.
18th	St. Luke the Evangelist, 1st cent.
19th	St. Frideswide, V. at Oxford, 8th cent.
	St. Eadnoth, B.M. of Dorchester, 1016.
20th	St. Bradan, C. in I.O.Man, 7th cent.
21st	St. Ursula and the Eleven Thousand Virgins, MM. at Cologne, 451.

22nd St. Salome, Mother of the Sons of Zebedee, 1st cent.
23rd St. Elfleda, W. at Glastonbury, Som., 10th cent.
      St. Columba, V.M. in Cornwall.
24th St. Cadfarch, C. at Penyos, Montgomery, 6th cent.
25th St. Marnoc, B. at Kilmarnock, Scotland.
      Sts. Canna, Sadwren and Crallo, CC. in Wales, 6th cent.
26th St. Eata, Ab. of Lindisfarne and B. of Hexham, 685.
      St. Tudyr, C. in Wales 7th cent.
      Sts. Gwynoc and Aneurin, CC. in Wales 6th cent.
27th Sts. Ia and Brecha, VV. in Cornwall, 6th cent.
      St. Odhran, Mk. at Iona, 563.
28th St. Dorbhen, Ab. of Iona, 713.
29th St. Elfleda, Abs. of Romsey, Hants. 1030.
      St. Marwinna, Abs. of Romsey, 993.
30th St. Arilda, V.M. at Kington, Thornbury, Glos.
      St. Illogan, C. in Cornwall.
31st St. Bee, Cumberland.

NOVEMBER
1st   Sts. Gwenfyl and Callwen, VV. at Llanddewi Brefi, Brecknock, 5th cent. Feast of All Saints.
2nd   St. Eve, B. of Slane, Ireland, 513.
3rd   St. Winefred, V.M. at Holywell, Flint, 7th cent.
4th   St. Brinstan, B. of Winchester, 934.
5th   St. Kenan, B. at Cleder, Brittany, 6th cent.
6th   St. Leonard, de Reresby, C. at Thrybergh, Yorks, 13th cent.
7th   St. Engelbert, B.M. at Cologne, 1225.
8th   St. Cuby, B. in Cornwall, 6th cent.
      St. Gernad, C. in Moray and Elgin, c. 934.
9th   St. Benignus, Abp. of Armagh, 468.
10th St. Justus, Abp. of Canterbury, c. 627.
11th St. Martin, B. of Tours, France, 400.
12th St. Cummian Fada, Ab. of Kilcomin, Ireland, 662.
13th St. Malcolm III, K. of Scotland, 1093.
      St. Brice, B. of Tours, 443.
14th St. Dubricius, Abp. of Caerleon, Wales, 524.
15th St. Maclovis, B. of Aleth, Brittany, 627.
16th St. Edmund, Abp of Canterbury, 1242.
17th St. Hugh, B. of Lincoln, 1200.
      St. Fergus, B. at Glamis, Scotland, 8th cent.
      St. Hilda, V. Abs. of Whitby, 679.
18th St. Wynnen, B. in Scotland, 579.
19th St. Elizabeth of Hungary, W. at Marburg, Germany, 1231.

20th   St. Edmund, K.M. at Bury St. Edmunds, Suffolk, 870.
21st   St. Albert, B.M. of Liege, Belgium, 1192.
22nd   St. Pragmatius, B. of Autun, c. 520.
23rd   St. Alexander Nevski, C. at Vladimir, Russia, 1263.
24th   St. Firmina, V.M. at Ameria, Italy, 303.
25th   St. Catherine, V.M. at Alexandria, 307.
26th   St. Innocent, B. of Irkutsk, Siberia, 1731.
       St. Leonard, of Port Maurice, O.M. at Rome, 1751.
27th   Sts. Facundus and Primitivus, MM. in Galicia, 304.
28th   St. Patrician, B. in Sutherland, 5th cent.
29th   Sts. Blasius and Demetrius, MM. at Veroli.
30th   St. Francis Xavier, S.J. at San-Chan, 1552.

DECEMBER
1st   St. Ansanus, M. at Siena, c. 303.
2nd   St. Trumwin, B. of the Picts, 686.
3rd   St. Birinus, B. of Dorchester, 654.
4th   St. Osmund, B. of Salisbury, 1099.
5th   St. Bassus, B.M. at Nice, France, 3rd cent.
6th   St. Nicholas, B. of Myra, Lycia, 4th cent.
7th   St. Agatho, M. at Alexandria, 250.
8th   St. Macarius, M. at Alexandria, 250.
9th   St. Lesmo, H. at Glentamire, Scotland.
10th   St. Deiniol, B. of Bangor, 7th cent.
11th   St. Barsabas, M. in Persia, 342.
12th   St. Finnian, B. of Clonard, Ireland, c. 552.
13th   St. Abra, V. at France, c. 400.
14th   Sts. Nicasius, B.M., and Eutropia, V.M. at Rheims, 407.
15th   St. Valerian, B.C. in Afica, 457.
16th   St. Bean, B. of Mortlach, Scotland, 1012.
17th   St. William Longsword, Duke M. at Rouen, 942.
18th   St. Flannan, B. of Kildare, Ireland, 7th cent.
19th   St. Samthana, Abs. of Clonebrone, Longford, Ireland, 8th cent.
20th   St. Philogonius, B. of Antioch, 323.
21st   St. Thomas, Ap. M. in India, 1st cent.
22nd   St. Ernan, Mk. of Drumhome, Donegal, 640.
23rd   St. Victoria, V.M. at Rome, 253.
24th   St. Gregory, M. at Spoleto, 303.
25th   St. Fulk, B. of Toulouse, 1231.
26th   St. Jarlath, B. of Tuam, Ireland, 560.
27th   St. John the Divine, Ap. at Ephesus, 101.
28th   St. Antony, Mk. at Lerins, 523.
29th   St. Thomas à Becket, Abp. at Canterbury, 1170.
30th   St. Anysius, B. of Thessalonica, c. 410.
31st   **St. Warembert, Ab. of Mont-St.-Martin, Cambrai, 1141.**